Ll ***STERDAY***

A Second ***nd Pictures***

Titles published by Llanteg Local History Society

Llanteg Down The Years (2000)
Llanteg: The Days Before Yesterday (2001)

LLANTEG: THE DAYS BEFORE YESTERDAY

MILLENNIUM FESTIVAL

Supported by the
Heritage Lottery Fund

LLANTEG: THE DAYS BEFORE YESTERDAY

A second memento of the village in words and pictures

Compiled by:

Ruth Roberts

Edited by:

Judith Lloyd

LLANTEG LOCAL HISTORY SOCIETY

Sandy-Grove, Llanteg, Narberth, Pembrokeshire, SA67 8QG, U.K.

First published in Great Britain 2001 by
LLANTEG LOCAL HISTORY SOCIETY
Sandy-Grove, Llanteg, Narberth, Pembrokeshire, SA67 8QG, U.K.

British Library Cataloguing-in-Publication Data.
A catalogue record for this book is available
from the British Library.

ISBN: 0-9538142-1-1

Printed by *Manuscript ReSearch Printing*
P.O. Box 33, Bicester, Oxon, OX26 4ZZ, U.K.
Tel: 01869 323447/322552 Fax: 01869 324096

PREFACE

Our first publication *Llanteg Down The Years* generated such interest that as a group we were encouraged to continue collecting information on our parish and its residents.

The lives of people in a small village in centuries past were inextricably linked with that of the village itself, so in continuing the story of Crunwere we will also be telling the story of our ancestors who lived here. They may long have since departed this life, but each of them in one way or another has helped to make us who we are.

This second volume follows closely the format of the first in that it contains more history on the parish of Crunwere and its people as well as additional reminiscences by locals.

We would like to express our appreciation to everyone who has helped with this publication, especially those who believed that they had nothing of value to contribute but who were often the ones who supplied us with some vital piece of information. Thanks also to all those who entrusted us with their treasured photographs, and to Tony Brinsden and John Tunster for again helping with proof reading. We are indebted to the National Lottery Heritage Board who generously provided us with a grant towards publication costs.

Regrettably, because *Llanteg Down The Years* was our first book there were some omissions and errors which we would like to rectify:-

1) We wish more adequately to express our appreciation for the invaluable start that Mr Charles F.Shepherd's book, *St. Elidyr, Crunwere - a Historical Note*, published originally in 1933, gave us in our research and which has also provided material on Crunwere Church which we have used in this book. Our thanks go to Mr Shepherd's family for allowing these extracts to be used, and we apologise that we inadvertently referred to him in the Bibliography as Dr Shepherd.

2) The late Margaret Hooper informed us that on page 51 in the third row

of the school photograph the 'three Hodge sisters' were not 'Bertha, Helen and ?' but 'Phylys, Ethel and Helen'.
3) Graham Mortimer has pointed out that on page 77 it was his grandfather, Tom Mortimer, who found Captain Jenkins's body in the pond, and not Tom Mortimer's grandfather.
4) On page 78: Mr Ken George has stated that his father, Mr Arthur George, was Hall Treasurer when it was first built. The contract for the building of the Hall went to Ellis and Richards, Wiseman's Bridge. The £25 to pay for the land was raised by public donations from the community. William Henry James built the kitchen which was at the end of the Hall.
5) On page 84: Mr Desmond Wolff would like to point out that strictly speaking culm is coal slack, although the word was often used to refer to the mixture of clay and coal slack. The large pit in which he used to bake potatoes as a child is roughly half-way between the two stiles in The Laurels Mountain, and would seem to be a natural geological feature. The clay pits were of course an entirely different feature, having been created by men with spades and were in the corner of the Mountain nearest the Chapel, and followed the line of Stoney Road.

Every effort has been made for accuracy in this second volume, but where personal reminiscences are concerned we have included them unaltered. We apologise in advance if there are any errors or omissions and we would appreciate that if any are found that they could be pointed out to us.

FOREWORD

To me the name 'Llanteg' means many things. As someone who was born and brought up in the village, it is my home and my heritage. My ancestors were brought up here and walked the same fields, roads and lanes that I have walked as a child. I think it is there that the similarity in my childhood and theirs ends.

I didn't have to walk to school after Crunwere C.P. School was closed in 1946, I had the luxury of being bussed to Amroth School, albeit in an old ex-Army personnel carrier. Thereafter during my schooldays I was always bussed to school. I left school at sixteen.

Just one generation earlier my uncle, who had won a place at Narberth Grammar School, was only able to attend by cycling the six or so miles each morning and night, summer and winter, regardless of the weather. Although a very good scholar, he had to leave at fourteen because he had to go out to work to help the family finances. My mother and aunty also had to leave school at fourteen and find employment.

If we go back a further generation in the Davies family, my grandfather left school at around twelve years of age and went out to work from that day.

A further generation back and my great-grandfather, John Davies, Greenacre, was sent into service at the age of nine years. His job was as a general messenger and handyman at Crunwere Rectory. Mind you, it was not absolutely all work and no play because it was there that he met his wife to be, Ann Richards from the parish of Cyffig, who was also employed there.

I was born during the first full year of the Second World War. Treats were few and far between, a couple of boiled sweets and you felt a million dollars. Everything including food and clothing was rationed, so it was a question of mend and make do.

Llanteg has always been famous for its 'characters'. I recall many of them. As a child I used to delight in listening to the tales told by these individuals round the supper table at haymaking and harvest times. Tales of tricks played on unsuspecting villagers, of gates moved around from one dwelling to another, and other harmless mischiefs as well as some that cannot be printed!

The village - like these reminiscences - has changed somewhat down the years, from a hamlet to an expanding community. Our Local History Society was only formed in the Spring of 1999. One book, *Llanteg Down the Years*, has already been published, but so much interesting information was gathered whilst compiling that book that it would have been shameful not to put it into print, and this second book is the result.

Tony Brinsden

CONTENTS

Part 3: Twentieth Century

PART ONE

VILLAGE HISTORY

MAP OF VILLAGE

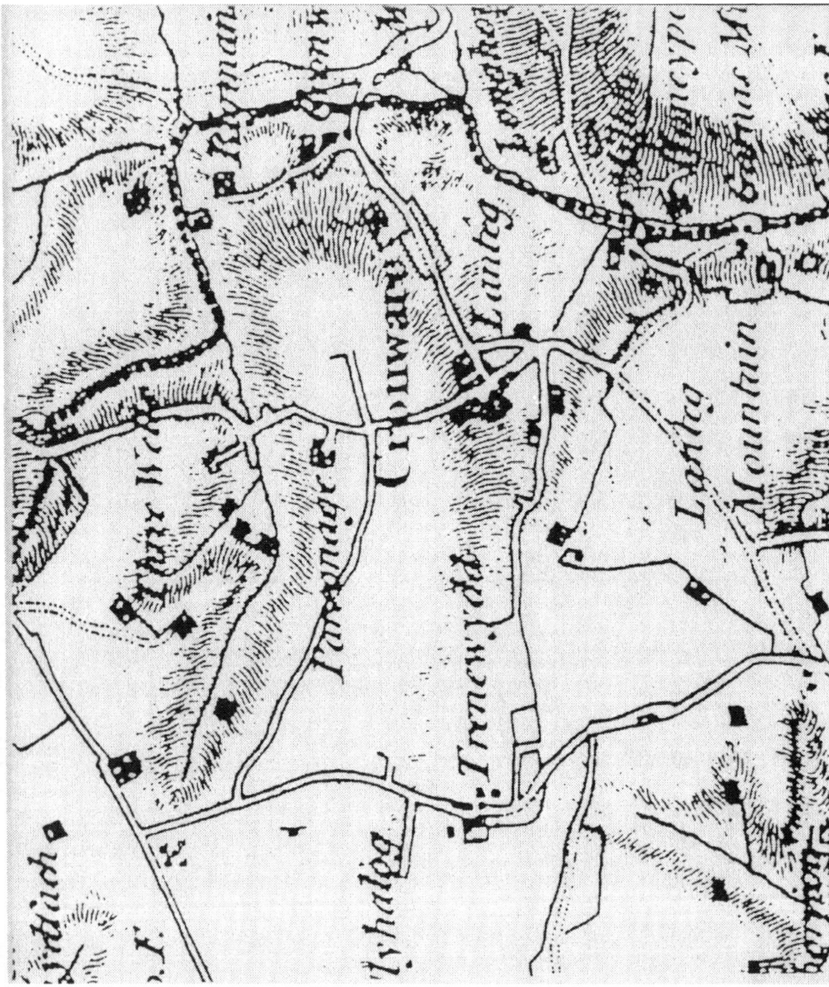

Ordnance Survey 1809

PART ONE: VILLAGE HISTORY

ORIGINS

Myths and legend conceal the story of the conversion of the Welsh people to Christianity. The fifth and sixth centuries witnessed a rapid expansion of Christian teaching throughout the British Isles, and Wales received this teaching from the missionaries of the early Celtic Church. They established a large number of religious settlements on or near the coasts of Wales. The prefix *Llan* in Welsh place names often indicates the location of an early Celtic church.

Life and Traditions in Rural Wales

Local author, Mr Roscoe Howells, believes that 'Teague' was a local name for Irishmen, often used in contempt, and that there are other examples of it in the area such as Teague's Dingle and Teague's Wood.

Size of Village

1563: 25 households

1670: 34 tax payers

1801: 44 families

Three Crunwere residents refusing to take the Oath of Allegiance to the Crown in the 1690s are recorded as Morris Davids, and the Rev. John Howell and his brother Robert.

Pembrokeshire County History Volume 111

An extract from George Owen's *Discription of Pembrokeshire*, written at the beginning of the 17th century, tells us: "...all Narberth hundred, excepting the parishes of Llanddewi and Lampeter (*Velfrey*) do speak the English". Mr Owen goes on to state, "There is also a waste and barren vein of land, beginning near Coedcanlas and running east to Templeton, Ludchurch, Crunwear and Amroth and so to the sea".

According to Brian John's *Pembrokeshire Past and Present*, the Plague or Black Death was in Pembrokeshire in 1651 and 1653. The worst affected areas were in and around Haverfordwest, but people died in all the villages to the south and east. The Plague was probably brought by sailors and spread quickly, usually killing its victims within three days.

One noteworthy feature produced by the limestone belts in this area is the formation of underground caves caused by the action of subterranean water. Where these caves are close to the surface the roofs may collapse, producing a pit or hollow in the ground known locally as 'pants', 'soakers' or 'soagers'. There are examples of these depressions in the fields to the rear of Middleton and surrounding area. One such 'soager' to the north of Middleton garden was used for rubbish, being apparently like a 'bottomless pit'.

On his *Historical Tour through Pembrokeshire* at the beginning of the 1800s Richard Fenton travelled close to Crunwere when he went from Amroth to Ludchurch and journied "through bad roads... in a county so full of attractions, and particularly in a neigbourhood where the genius of hospitality every where holds out the most undisguised invitations... I proceed with difficulty".

The *Acreage Returns of Wales 1801* lists Crunwere as 'a very small parish' with the following land being cultivated:- wheat (24 acres), barley (59), oats (80), potatoes (7) and turnips (2).

CRUNWERE CHURCH

In the Middle Ages most people stood in the nave during church services. The expression 'the weak to the wall' comes from the practice of providing a stone bench for the infirm around the walls of the nave. Wooden benches were introduced in the first half of the 14th century. In most churches only the wealthier inhabitants provided their own seats, and most parishioners remained standing well after the Reformation. During the 17th century churches were furnished with pews. The owners or tenants of the largest farms sat in a position of prominence at the front.

Oxford Companion to Local History 1996.

Some churches now appear isolated because the village that lay close alongside them has decayed and disappeared. If a church is situated oddly in relation to a village, it is likely that the main focus of settlement has altered over the centuries. This is what may have happened at Crunwere. Dyfed Archaeological Trust believes that the evidence from aerial photographs suggests that there was an ancient settlement in the field to the west of the church driveway.

Alternatively some churches occupy what now appear to be odd sites because they were deliberately sited to convert adherents from pagan forms of religion.

Crunwere Church has a well in the field to the north and this may have had significance in years past. Many a well had a long and useful history before it was sanctified for Christian use. Former pagan wells, once they were blessed and sanctified by Christian priests, acted as supplies of Holy Water for the fonts. Numerous wells retained into modern times their reputation for curing the sick.

Yew trees were also customarily planted near the church gate (as in Crunwere). This is confirmed by a reference in the 12th century *Book of Llandaff*, where it clearly stated that sanctuary would be available for "those who sought it between the yew tree and the church door". Also in the *Book of Llandaff* is reference to 'Lann Cronnguern' which may suggest a pre-conquest foundation for Crunwere Church.

Crunwere Church 1870s **Photo:Eirwen Davies**

The church consists of a nave (32ft by 18ft), chancel (15ft by 12ft), north transept (14ft by 11ft), south transept (14ft by 11ft) and a western tower (17ft north and south by 16ft east and west). It was rebuilt in 1843 (when the south transept was added) and restored in 1878, with the exception of the tower and north transept. The tower is of the traditional 'Pembrokeshire' type and consists of three storeys, the lowest one having a plain vault. The tower is lighted by narrow loops. The west door is blocked and the window above is modern, as is the font.

Visited 20th May 1915,
Acct to the Royal Commission on Ancient Monuments

In 1480 it appears that the Abbot of St Albans Monastery was patron of several rectories and vicarages in Pembrokeshire, including 'Rectoria de Cranwer'.

1480 Account to St Albans Monastery

According to the *Topographical Dictionary of Wales* in 1834 Cronwere *(sic)* was six miles E.S.E. of Narberth and had 274 inhabitants. It was situated a short distance south of the Turnpike road from Laugharne to Narberth (*via Tavernspite*). An average annual expenditure amounting to £58 6s was applied for the maintenance of the poor.

In 1847, in an *Account on the State of Education in Wales*, the following information was included for the parish of Cronware *(sic)*: "The Rev. W. D. Phillips, Vicar, informed me that the Labourers' wages with food are from 9d to 10d per day; without food 1s, and 1s 3d in winter. Farm servants £5 to £9 and female servants £3 to £7 per year. Masons and Carpenters 1s 10d to 2s on their own provisions, and 1s 2d with food".

Written by William Morris, Asst, 4th December 1846.

According to the Dyfed Archeaological Trust Crunwere Church is of limestone rubble construction; there are suspended floors in 60% of the church, below floor heating in 5% (nave) and possibly a cellar beneath 15% (the vent in the south wall of the south transept may lead to an underground chamber inserted in 1878). This medieval church is central within an earthwork of a disappeared medieval village site. The tiled floors date from 1878 and the tower from the mid-16th century. The south porch was rebuilt in 1878 on the site of an earlier porch. The 1878 renovations cost £550. The carved rood beam, with the Holy Family figures, is from the 19th century, as may be the pulpit. The font is probably from 1878.

The following records remain for the church and are available for consultation in the Haverfordwest Record Office:

Baptisms from 1783
Marriages from 1754
Burials from 1783.

Mr Charles F. Shepherd, writing in *St. Elidyr, Crunwere - a Historical Note* (1933) gives us much information about the church. There are four churches dedicated to St. Elidyr in Pembrokeshire: Crunwere, Amroth, Ludchurch and Stackpole Elidor. Fenton in his *Tour through Pembrokeshire* states that these churches were founded by Sir Elidwr de Stackpool. In an early charter, mention is made of Crunwere being given to St. Teilo of Llandaff, and the Episcopal registers of 1486 give it as the parish church of St. Teilo. Mr Shepherd thought that it was quite possible that 'Elidyr' was only a misspelling of 'Eliud', another name for Teilo. In former times parishioners would hold a special service once a year in honour of the Saint to which their church was dedicated (*St. Teilo was born at Pen Alun, modern day Penally, in the sixth century and his saint's day became the 9th of February*).

The east window is of stained glass and is in three parts, depicting the Crucifixion in the centre, the Ascension on the left and the Resurrection on the right. It was given by Mrs Georgiana Morgan of Heatherland in memory of her husband, Rev. Richard Morgan (a son of Trenewydd). The Ten Commandments are inscribed on the walls on either side of this window.

The church has an Elizabethan chalice, of the 'Amroth type', its ornamentation corresponding exactly with that of the Amroth chalice. There is decoration around the bowl which has the following inscription:-

POCVLVM*ECLESIE*DE*CROVNWARE

Underneath the foot is roughly scratched: E de Cronwer 8½oz. This would have included the weight of the cover, now sadly lost. The only mark is that of the makers, one that is found on much of the church plate in Pembrokeshire. The date, according to this mark, is put at 1574-87. Apart from this there is another chalice, a paten and a flagon, all of plated metal.

The following are extracts of tablets which are found in the church:

North transept - *Thomas Davies late of Landteague Esq. who departed this life Apr. 13 1706 aged 98.*

North side of nave - *Hugh Slader Glanville, 24th Welsh Regiment, who died at Gaza of wounds received in Battle, November 11, 1917, aged 25. Interred at Beersheba. R.I.P.*

South wall of nave - *Augusta Louisa, youngest and dearly loved daughter of Lloyd and Maria Philipps, Oakland, in this Parish, who died the 31 July, 1892, aged 25 years. Thy will be done.*

Near the above - *Talbot Davies, son of John and Ann Davies 'Greenacre' in this Parish, who died April 15, 1907, aged 32 years. Interred at Mount Pleasant Cemetery, Seattle, U.S.A.*

South transept - *of Ann, 4th daughter of Rob't and Eliz'th Morgan of Trenewed in this Parish who died Jan. 6, 1826, aged 8 years.*
(The story has been handed down via Mrs Catherine Phillips, Middleton, from her predecessors that on the day Ann was buried the snow was so deep that the little coffin had to be carried over the fields from Trenewydd to the church, a journey of possibly a mile and a half.)
Chancel, south side - *Ann, wife of the rev'd Thom's Dalton, Rec't of this parish obt. Jany, 29, 1815, AEtat 76 ys, ALSO of their Daughter obit May 26, 1818 AETat sue 41ys. ALSO OF their son John, Gent. Surgeon, obit May 26, 1822 AEtat sui 41ys.*
Porch - *Benjamin Griffiths of Lanteague in this Parish who died Dec. 17, 1854 aged 54 years.* (The stone was removed from its grave when the south entrance was reinstated and the west door blocked up.)
On the outside of the Church - *near this wall lies the Body of John Howell A.M. the Son of Reynold Howell of Trenewyed, Gent. he was sometime Rector of New Radnor but in the year of Trial 1691 was deprived of all that he could not keep with a good conscience. Who died Jan. 17, 1727, aged 70.* (A stone tablet in memory of a non-juring clergyman.)

Crunwere Church Interior 1870s **Photo: Eirwen Davies**

As stated in the *Oxford Companion to Local History* (O.U.P. 1996), from the 1840s onwards the High Church movement dictated how the interiors of churches should be arranged. The present interior appearance of most ancient parish churches dates from the period 1840-1890, when box pews and galleries were removed. This is exactly what happened at Crunwere when the church was renovated in the 1870s.

Mr Charles F. Shepherd also compiled a list of incumbents that he had been able to trace *(those after the 1980s have been added)*:

1344 Simon Johan	1349 Richard Portyn
1407 Thomas Bron	1407 James Vayner
1486 John David	1486 John Tudor
1534 Griffin Lloid	1554 Nicholas Nicols
1631 Humphrey Smart	1703 Charles Williams
1755 Thomas Williams	1783 Thomas Dalton
1830 Davis Jones	1839 William Davies Phillips
1886 William Garner	1907 Richard Roberts Jones
1917 Evan Davies	1923 Robert Jackett
1934 Daniel Morgan	1948 Isambard George Horatio Bowen-Harries
1955 D. G. Lloyd Jones	1958 David Stanley Hobbs
1979 John Burrenston Lewis	1987 David Williams
1995 Nicholas Cale	

In 1970 Crunwere was united with Amroth, and in 1979 Crunwere united with Ludchurch and Templeton. In 1984 there was an interregnum of three years until in 1987 Crunwere and Ludchurch were finally united with Begelly.

To commemorate the new millennium, church bells were rung across the country at 12 noon on January 1st 2000. At Crunwere this task was performed by Alan and Andrew Mason of Carlands, Llanteg.

ZOAR CHAPEL

Zoar Deacons 1950s Photo: Elizabeth Hall

Back Row, L. to R: *W. E. Mathias, W. J. V. Davies, W. J. Thomas, M. R. Raymond, A. G. Phillips.*

Front Row, L. to R: *G. Wilfred Davies, Rev. Charles Vaughan, W. E. Harries.*

Mr Glyn James, Woodview, has in his possession a booklet published in 1954 to commemorate the centenary of both Zoar Baptist Church, Llanteg, and Hebron Baptist Church, Saundersfoot - *A Century of Witness Completed*. In this booklet part of the story of Zoar is explained as follows:

Originally the Baptists worshipped in a grain loft at Long Lane Farm, occupied by Tom Phillips. Eventually a place of worship was erected. The church cost about £60 to build and afterwards one of the founders, John Morgan, added a two-roomed lean-to as a caretaker's cottage, at a cost of £20. Mr Morgan charged the church £1 per year interest on the money he had laid out, until John Phillips the Corner organised a few concerts and with the proceeds bought the property from Robert, the son of John Morgan.

Architecturally, Zoar is of a rather peculiar shape and form. From the middle of the floor space the seats form a 'rising gallery' which of course increases the seating capacity. The seats are from the original Baptist

Church at Molleston, one of the oldest Baptist Churches in Pembrokeshire.

In 1935 a porch and entrance gate were erected in memory of the late Mr and Mrs Griffith Harries and their son Tom Harries, by the surviving children. The seat in the porch was made and presented by the late Mr Lewis Thomas, Amroth.

ANCIENT REMAINS

Although we have no castles or other obvious historical ruins in Llanteg, the following are ancient features that have been recorded by the Dyfed Archaeological Trust:

Parc Garw, Parc Garn - may have contained a Bronze Age round barrow? (*field north of Crosslands Road*).

Lime Kilns - at the quarries north of Milton and south of Trenewydd.

St. Elidyr's Church - medieval/post-medieval building.

Llanteg Common - common land, medieval/post-medieval. 0.4 acre area, heath, unlimited public access (*south of A477 opposite Crofty Nursery*).

King's Piece - a field which was once Crown land? (*S. W. of Broomylake*).

Bleanhafod - earthwork, circular enclosure in field.

Hollow Way - medieval/post-medieval (?) earthwork (*in field S.W. of Trenewydd Farm*).

Little Newhouse - earthwork/enclosure, "D" shaped (queried as an antiquity) (*south of the Lime Road*).

Llanteg Enclosure - Hillfort (?) 0.23 acre, Iron Age circular earthwork/ enclosure, bank and ditch. It was partially examined in 1984 when the road was being widened. The bank at the western side of the enclosure was of a uniform clay loam soil with a darker layer lower down, possibly indicating a former ground surface (*where Blackheath and the A477 are now situated*).

Llanteg - the name of a group of post-medieval buildings, a settlement (*comprising East and West Llanteg, Fern Villa and Ashdale*). There are also old quarries nearby.

Trelissy (just outside parish boundary) - a roughly circular ringwork enclosing a stone-built rectangular structure. It was partly excavated in the early 1950s and is believed to have been a Romano-British homestead. Occupied from the early 2nd century A.D. to at least the 3rd century A.D. The earthwork has now largely been ploughed out. A spindle whorl, pottery, tile, large stud, lead and iron slag are in the Tenby museum (*about a quarter of a mile south of Trelissy farm*).

PART TWO

NINETEENTH CENTURY

PART TWO: NINETEENTH CENTURY

BEN PRICE'S RECOLLECTIONS

Ben Price was a local boy who spent his childhood during the 1850s and '60s at various places in the area, including Rhydgoch, Garness and Greenacre. In later years while living in London he submitted numerous articles to the *Narberth Weekly News* entitled 'South East Corner of Pembrokeshire 60 Years and More Ago'. These articles vividly captured life in the locality around the middle of the 19th century. The following are extracts from Mr Price's writings relating to Crunwere, the parish where he grew up.

Tenby Market

After 1860, Mr Price's father, who had been working in Cardiff, was sent home to Greenacre very ill with a fever. His life was in danger and for a full year he was unable to support his family (a wife and six healthy children under ten years old). However, his wife faced the problem with "a cheerful smile on her face", and set about buying poultry, eggs, butter etc., taking them generally twice a week to Tenby market to sell.

Mrs Price collected her wares from the parishes of Lampeter, Cyffig and Eglwyscymmin where she was well known from her youth and where she had many family connections and friends. Except on market days she would be travelling the rough and muddy roads and lanes between farms and cottages in search of produce. She was out in all weathers, often unsuitably or insufficiently clad, sometimes on foot and sometimes with a donkey to carry her, or a donkey cart. Before market she would be up late into the night, killing, feathering and trussing the poultry and preparing her goods. In the morning she had the nine-mile walk or donkey cart ride to Tenby. Then in the late afternoon she would tramp the town offering her unsold goods from door to door at knock-down prices. This done she made what purchases she could afford (plus a few 'lozenges' for the children) then would find three or four women neighbours on similar business and they would start for home together, each on their donkey's back.

Robert Bevlin's Wedding

Tommy Menns was about thirty years old, a man with the simplicity of a child of three and the harmlessness of a lamb. He lived under the charge of Tommy Evans and his wife at Donkey Hill, a lonely cottage in the valley below Goitre, and he was always dressed in corduroy, which was invariably clean but always short of buttons so that various pieces were held together with string or pieces of thorn. He could be depended upon to do any errand Mrs Evans wanted, and to carry out her instructions carefully, but Ben Price writes that he never saw Tommy Menns do any physical tasks, even though he believed Tommy to be in good health.

One morning when young Ben was at Billy Oriel's school at the Toll Gate *(Llanteg Cross)* they were astonished to see a procession of about twelve gaily-dressed people marching in pairs down the hill towards them, with Tommy Menns at their head. He was decked out with coloured ribbons fastened to his hat, shoulders, elbows, wrists and knees, and was marching with all the pride of a high-stepping horse. (*This could possibly have been a relic of the old custom of having a village 'bidder' who would visit all the houses in the neighbourhood to invite them to a wedding feast. The bidder would be attired in clothing especially suited to the occasion, and carried in his hands a white stick of office decorated with ribbons of all colours - 'Life and Traditions in Rural Wales'*.)

This was the wedding party of Robert Davies, Bevlin. Mr Price was at the party in the evening at Bevlin and writes of the dinner with the guests around the table, and of the dancing which was held later in a building to the south of the main dwelling. 'Tom the Cabin', wearing a tall hat was playing the fiddle. 'Robert a Bevelin' was, like his brother Lewis, a gifted singer. Tragically, he was to die within a few years of his wedding (*aged 31 in May 1865*).

Allen Palmer - Butcher

Allen Palmer had originally been landlord of The Golden Lion *(now The Laurels)* but the place ceased to trade as an inn sometime in the 1840s and Mr Palmer set up a butcher's shop in what had been the public room. Unfortunately he remained very fond of beer and would go to Tavernspite as often as possible, never returning without being inebriated. When sober he was a quiet, inoffensive man, but when not sober (although Ben Price never heard of any harm he did) he would strike terror into the local children with his shouting and threatening behaviour. Poor Mr Palmer eventually paid the penalty for his drunken habits by drowning in the little shallow brook just below the bridge at Amroth (*January 1871 aged 58 years*).

His wife Martha was the daughter of the former Rector of Crunwere, the Rev. Thomas Dalton. She attended markets and fairs to buy livestock and would take the butchered carcasses to sell at the weekly markets. Young Ben Price often went with her in the cart to St Clears and on the way would watch for omens of good or bad luck such as how many magpies (or 'payats') were seen. He recalls that they would have to drive the animals - mostly calves - home afterwards. As soon as the calves were bought, some expert in attendance at the market would bleed them in the neck, then close up the edges of the wound with an ordinary pin. Mr Price had to drive the calves in this condition all along the Turnpike road from St Clears to Lanteague (*sic*), a distance of six or seven miles. The animals would be very weak and he would have to urge them unmercifully. Two or three that had collapsed would be put in the cart for the rest of the way, while others would have to be left at the roadside. Mr Price recalls that the cruelty of this practice did not strike them at the time since they were only doing what everyone else did.

Parson Phillips

The Rev. William Davies Phillips, rector of Crunwere and vicar of Amroth *(1839-1886)*, was held in very high respect, being known to all as 'Parson Phillips'. He had several fine white horses which he generally rode when performing his duties. He would pass young Ben Price's house (*Greenacre, now a ruin*) every Sunday, and frequently on weekdays - "I imagine I can see him now jogging along near Longlane holding a white cane".

He gave the children the impression that he was severe but he enjoyed a joke: when Mr Price was about eight and living at Rhydgoch (*old homestead on road near Broomylake entrance*) Parson Phillips visited London, and in his absence young Ben remarked that "the Parson would then see where babies came from". Soon after his return Mr Phillips called to visit, and Ben remembers his mother telling the Rector what the boy had said. "His face lit up with merriment, ho ho ho he laughed" - and then he had trotted off on his mare, chuckling until out of hearing.

Around 1860 Rev. Phillips and his family received a dreadful shock with the death of their eldest son, 'Master Johnny', whilst away at school (*John Charles Phillips died in March 1860 whilst in Dorset aged 16 years*).

Mr Price remembers being in Crunwere Church some little time after the burial, when he believed the Parson was taking the service for the first time after his great trial, that he broke down in his sermon, overcome with emotion. The whole parish was in the deepest mourning, for everyone felt for the Parson and his family, and 'Master Johnny' had himself been very well liked. The only other similar experience of general sorrow was when the Duke of Clarence, brother of the King, died *(the Duke of Clarence ascended the throne as William IV in 1830, dying in 1837)*. The latter affected a wider circle of people, but at the time the parish was their world.

Sheep Minding

Ben Price was living at Rhydgoch when William Raymond (his cousin) of West Llanteg came and told him that his sheep had broken into the Parson's turnips. As Will couldn't mend the 'slop' in the hedge until evening he wanted young Ben - who was about eight years old at the time - to watch them in the afternoon and guard the field (which was on the right as you left the Parsonage (*The Rectory - now Crunwere House*) going to Llanteg, the Parson's turnips being in the field to the west). Mr Price said he did his job "zealously" for some time, but as it was a hot summer's day and the field faced south, his interest began to flag and soon he was fast asleep.

The next thing he knew was Allen Palmer, the butcher from The Golden Lion (*The Laurels*) shouting from the top corner of the field, having spotted the boy lying there as he was on his way down the hill. Young Ben forgot all about his cousin's sheep and as soon as Mr Palmer had gone he scampered off home, convinced that he had slept for days - and nothing his mother could say could persuade him that it was the same day.

He afterwards learnt that while he lay sleeping the sheep had come past him and enjoyed a good feed of the Parson's turnips. He commented that he had "proved utterly unworthy of trust!"

'Davie The Cabin'

Anne and David Evans lived at the Cabin, at the lower corner of Marros Mountain. One day Mrs Evans came to ask about getting Tom (Ben Price's elder brother by two years) to come as farm boy and general helper on their out-of-the-way farm. Because Ben Price's mother needed help with her huckstering *(pedlar's)* business, she had already arranged for the two boys to attend Amroth School on alternate weeks; but young Ben Price volunteered to work at the Cabin and was so persistent that he got the job instead of his brother.

It was a little after the Christmas of 1863 and he was to spend four or five months there - "the most bitter and miserable time I ever passed through, before or since".

The daily work consisted of feeding and cleaning out the two horses, three or four cows and other animals, and visiting and counting numerous sheep that roamed over Marros Mountain and which "always took full advantage of their liberty". The boy would then have to go to a certain part of the mountain with a hook and wooden fork to cut enough furze for the horses, tie it down into a bundle, then carry it on his shoulders to the shed where the chaffcutter was housed and where he would be "straining for what seemed like an interminable time" turning the handle to produce enough chaff for the horses that night. After this he would have to fetch in, tie up, and feed the various other animals. Anne Evans's son Phillip was two or three years younger than Ben Price and would occasionally be put to help.

In the summer, David Evans, a very hard-working man, took charge of one of the lime kilns at Blaencilgoed, as he did each year. During the season he would be at the kiln continuously day and night attending to the burning of the limestone, taking snatches of sleep in his little cabin when he could. Young Ben Price would go daily from the Cabin to Blaencilgoed, starting very early in the morning, with food for Mr Evans and himself. He would stay to help during the day, returning to the Cabin at night - which meant leaving at dawn and returning at twilight or dark. Though he rode a donkey, he says he was so tired on the return journey that he often slept on the donkey's back.

Once a week on Sunday afternoons the boy would go home to his mother and would be able to have a change of clothing. One particular Sunday he lay down on the settle and soon fell fast asleep. He began having such bad dreams about his work and grew so agitated and feverish that his mother told him "ya shenna go back to the Cabin any more, boy".

David Evans had to work very hard to eke out a living from his little farm and pay his rent. Ben Price tells us that Mr Evans held the mistaken and often expressed belief that "hard work never killed anyone", though he himself personally believed that the overstraining of the strength of the young was responsible for many a stunted growth and premature death.

David Evans was known as 'Awl Davie the Cabin', because he was taken to be older than he actually was. He was wrinkled and absolutely toothless, and despite being unsteady and somewhat bent, was tough and very active. He was, as Mr Price understood, one of the founders of the little Baptist Chapel at Zoar, Llanteg; and although he was quite illiterate, he knew a great deal of the contents of the Bible. He would spend his evenings after dark sitting in the corner by the fire in the lower room, knitting stockings, and perhaps singing hymns with a very "inharmonious voice". At a certain time his wife would read a chapter or psalm in Welsh, whereupon they would then sing a hymn together, and Mr Evans would pray fervently before retiring to bed after a supper which invariably "consisted of budram with unleavened barley bread and probably a little cheese". He was an inveterate chewer of tobacco, never without his 'quid' rolling about in his mouth and being squeezed between his toothless gums until everything around him would be "sprinkled and spluttered and stained by the strong liquor". David Evans was by no means alone in his habit in those days: men and boys would vie with each other as to how copiously they could squirt the dark brown saliva from between their teeth and how far and accurately they could shoot it.

David Evans was a faithful member of Zoar and a regular attender at all meetings there. On Sundays, like most others of his class, he would wear his best corduroy breeches and leggings and a kind of brown homespun coat. He also had a fondness (as did other old men Ben Price knew) for a red waistcoat made of some material in "imitation of fur" (*probably brushed flannel*).

David Evans was a strangely mixed character in which the hard struggle for an honest living and a religious zeal predominated.

'A Daughter of Trenewydd' - Jane Morgan of Oaklands.

by Ben Price, extracted from the Narberth Weekly News, January 17th 1924.

Miss Jane Morgan was a middle-aged lady about the time I knew her first, and lived at the Oaklands. She was the daughter of Trenewydd, and owned or held on lease a small estate, and was surrounded by half a dozen or more smallholders who were her tenants, over whom she deservedly exercised considerable influence for good. I imagine she was not wealthy, even on the scale of those days, but she was most ladylike in her mode of life and behaviour, and must have been endowed with superior intelligence and good sense, and lived an exemplary life amongst her own people.

One of the first things I remember in connection with her is being present at a singing school in her kitchen when she was teaching us to sing 'Little child, do you love Jesus, oh how He loves' to the old Welsh tune of *Ar hyd y nos*, and her pitch fork was one of her own table forks. I also remember about that time being one of a company of children taken by her to Yerewere (Amroth) when we had to take our own cups or mugs with us, and we were given tea and cake on the Black Rock, the water boiled over a fire lit in one of the sheltered corners of that fine picnicking spot.

'Miss Jane', as she was called, kept a servant man as well as a maid. The man's name was Dick - I don't know his surname *(he was Richard Thomas)* - and he was groom, gardener, ploughman, and everything else. For two seasons, at least, when I was between nine and eleven years of age, I was employed to assist Dick in hoeing turnips, cleaning and transplanting mangolds, and doing any other odd jobs I was capable of, and my pay was fourpence a day, providing my own food. Our cupboard was bare enough at home in those days, and I shall ever remember that many a meal was surreptitiously given me by the sympathetic maid; and I confidently trust and believe that when that maid *(perhaps Jane James)* will have to render an account on that Great Day for her acts done in the body, the all-knowing and just Judge will hold her guiltless for having had compassion on a hungry child (for I was nothing more) even though it was in part at the cost of her mistress.

'Miss Jane' had a niece, an exceedingly pretty girl of about my own age, who was a frequent visitor at the Oaklands *(Emma Morgan)*. She, like her aunt, was ladylike and superior, and without being arrogant or haughty, knew how to hold the position becoming her station in life, and consequently did not allow familiarities on the part of those beneath her in the social scale. But one day when hay was being led, I was helping as far as I could on the hayrick, and this young girl joined us in the merry spirit which seemed to animate all haymaking and haymakers in those days. Urged by this spirit, I - greatly daring - gave Miss a thoroughly good rolling and tossing in the hay, which to my great relief she did not at all resent but appeared to enjoy.

I have heard recently that this young girl, now an elderly lady, still lives in Pembrokeshire, and if she by any chance should read these notes I wish her and all hers, as I do all the readers of the Narberth 'Weekly News', a very happy and prosperous New Year.

The census of 1861 shows the house servants at that date to be Jane James and Richard (Dick) Thomas. In 1881, the census shows Jane

Morgan, aged 58, as head of the household, and Mary Davies as maidservant. Miss Jane is buried in Crunwere churchyard; her dates are April 26 1822 - May 4 1884.

Miss Jane's niece Emma Morgan - the 'exceedingly pretty girl' mentioned above by Ben Price - lived at Heatherland. She and her sister, Catherine, were the daughters of the Rev. Richard Morgan (of Trenewydd), vicar of Aberavon and Bagland, who had died at the age of 42 in 1851.

Llanteg 'Bandy'

extracted from the Narberth Weekly News, 11th October 1923

At Billy the Gate's school *(in the tollhouse at Llanteg crossroads)* we sat on backless forms, had no desks, no blackboard, no maps or pictures, nor any of the now essential equipment of the meanest school in the country; no sanitary provision, no playground except the turnpike roadway, on which we played marbles, cricket, or any other game in season known to us.

The method of our game of cricket, or 'bandy' as we called it, was very primitive and is worth describing. We selected sides as cricketers do now, and one side bowled and fielded, whilst the others were at the wicket. Scoring was done by us then as it is now, i.e., after hitting the ball you had to run from wicket to wicket, but we generally had a rule that if you 'tipped' the ball you must run (a rule if adopted in modern cricket would make high scores very scarce). Another rule generally adopted by us was that if you hit the ball over the hedge alongside the road you were out, therefore, there were no boundary hits to claim credit for, but much to the contrary, as, of course, you were out if the ball disturbed your 'wicket', or if the ball was caught in its flight after you had hit it, or if the ball was returned to the 'wicket' before you reached it.

The 'wicket' consisted of two stones a little less in height that the diameter of the ball; these were set on the ground 15 to 18 inches apart, and a light twig laid upon them from one to the other. The stones were selected so that they afforded the least possible resting-place for the twig in order that the least touch by the ball would knock it off. The 'bat' was a bent stick, after the shape of a hockey stick, cut out of the hedge, or wherever one of the necessary shape could be found, and it was known to us as a 'bandy'. The ball was generally made of rag or yarn wound up as tightly as we could, and perhaps covered with canvas or cloth sewn on as a cover. It was a matter of honour that the ball should be trundled along the ground, not pitched to the wicket, so 'overhand' bowling was out of the question;

the batsman, on the other hand, was expected to hit the ball with a clear stroke, not with a sweeping motion along the ground - girls only were permitted to do this, for we had to allow the girls to join us in the game owing to lack of sufficient boys in the school.

I wonder if this kind of cricket is ever played, even in the most outlandish corner of the country, nowadays.

Football we never had. Athletics of any and all kinds were entirely unknown to us, and bathing and swimming were tabooed, even had there been opportunities for this, then considered unnecessary, exercise.

Mr Benjamin Morris of Lanteague Farm

extracted from the Narberth Weekly News, October 11th 1923

Many of the features and circumstances of that time *(the author's childhood)* stand out clearly in my memory, from the cone-bearing fir tree by the side of the road leading to the mountain; the swallows that built their mud nests under the eaves of the roof; the travellers along the turnpike road, amongst whom I distinctly remember a wounded soldier partly in uniform who had returned from the then recently terminated 'Roosian' War *(the Crimean War, 1853-6)*.

One of the first persons to attract my notice amongst the people of the place was Mr Benjamin Morris, of Lanteague Farm. He was then approaching probably his 70th year, and was crippled by what I understand was rheumatism; at any rate, he was very lame, leaning to one side as he walked, supported by a stout staff in one hand, whilst the other was laid akimbo on the projecting hip on the other side. He was dressed in good homespun cloth and knee breeches and grey stockings, without leggings, and low shoes, and with a crowned top hat upon his head. His face was round and firm and regular, with a little side whiskers, as was the fashion at the time. His figure was of average height, of stiff build, and the impression I have of him is that of a strong, firm, but kindly and good natured man, and his portrait would be very near to that of the conventional John Bull. He was at that time always accompanied by a big dog, called, I believe, either 'Bell' or 'Bess', that could always control a bull inclined to be ferocious belonging to her master. Mr Morris would often in passing a little group of us children, with a pleasant smile greet us with:-

"Jim Crow's sister's name was Mary Anne,
She could ride a donkey as well as any man,
Jump about and wheel about and do just so,
Jump about and wheel about and jump Jim Crow".

Or:-

"Little Mary Anne,

Playing with the sand,

With a big piece of white bread and butter in her hand".

Or some other droll saying which he thought likely to interest or amuse us. Many years after that, when I was approaching manhood, and he had reached the confines of old age, I have sat for hours at the fireside in the interesting old farmstead of Lanteague, listening with the greatest interest to his stories of his youth and of my grandfather, Morris Price, and his family connections. The two families, 100 or more years ago, had been closely associated socially, but through the veins of the present descendants of Mr Benjamin Morris there runs blood nearly akin to my own.

(Mr Benjamin Morris, born in the parish of Llansadurnan in either 1785 or 1786, first appears in the Crunwere census in 1841, where he is recorded as a farmer of 160 acres. He subsequently appears in the censuses of 1851, 1861 and 1871; but by 1881 it is his eldest son, Richard, who is recorded as head of the household.)

Billy the Gate

extracted from the Narberth Weekly News, April 19th 1923 and October 11th 1923

At Llanteague the then new turnpike road to Hobbs Point crosses the two old roads, one from Tavernspite, and the other from the church and beyond, where they joined, and then immediately separated again - one for Trenewydd etc., and the other for the direction of Amroth. At this point there was a gate across the new road, which you could not pass with any vehicle, horse, ass etc., without paying a certain toll (*a list of prices is given in the Appendix*). In connection with this gate, and built up to it on one side of the road, there was a little house of two floors with a hipped and slated roof, with a window at each side on the ground floor to enable the occupant, who was the collector of the toll, to watch the traffic up and down the road. There was a door in two heights looking across the road, and a window in the upper floor right over it. I am dependent on memory, but I judge the building was not more than 12 feet by 12 feet out to out.

In this little house the toll collector lived. At the time I want to refer to, this office was held by a bachelor of peculiar parts and appearance named William Oriel, known locally as 'Billy the Gate'. In addition to this public position, he was a cobbler, and made and mended boots and shoes, and besides kept in his little house above described a school for the instruction of youth in the rudiments of knowledge. This at that time was the only school in the parish, and was attended by about twenty children between four and perhaps ten years of age, who were taught the alphabet, a little spelling, reading, and a little - very little - writing, mostly on a slate. It is no discredit to the pluralist head teacher to add that this covered the curriculum of his capacity, for it represented the extent of his opportunities in that direction, and he did not attempt to go beyond his depth.

His peculiar appearance was due to a severe curvature of the spine, which gave him an undue proportion of length of leg, and shortness of body, and set his head unusually low between his shoulders. This also was no discredit to him, but on the contrary appealed to everybody for sympathy and consideration, as it arose from some accident or weakness or neglect during his infancy. He was a strict disciplinarian, and I can even now feel the bitter sting of his ebony ruler on the palm of my hand, and of his cobbler's knee-strap across my shoulders, and I am honestly convinced that I was not by any means an unruly little boy.

To this academy of learning my brother Tom and I were introduced in the summer of 1856 walking daily from the Roses, where my parents then lived, but my father had taken Garness Mill, and was entering into possession in September. I was then four and a half years old.

We were probably 20 children or thereabouts attending this school, each paying a penny a week for the privilege, finding his or her own slate, pencil, spelling book, etc., and were drawn from eight or ten households in the parish. I often wonder what has become of them. I don't think I have met more than four of them since we were children. They are scattered in many directions, and the majority are in all likelihood laid beneath the sod by now.

Millers and Blacksmiths

extracted from the Narberth Weekly News, June 21st 1923

My brother and I entered Billy Oriel's educational establishment at Lanteague Gate in 1856, walking from the Red Roses - a long distance for children so young as we were then - but we had an excellent road, and our journey was broken about halfway, for the new dwelling-house at Castle Ely Mill was then being built, and father was working upon it as a carpenter. I remember endeavouring to climb the ladder to the upper floor before the stairs were built, and failing in the attempt, and I remember Jemmy, the stoutish and elderly miller, who then lived in the old house attached to the mill building, with the entrance on the lower level. Benny, a son of 'Johnny the Welshman', who lived at Crafty, was Jemmy's boy, and he ultimately became Jemmy's successor as miller.

In that year, 1856, my father had agreed to take Garness Mill, and in due course we went to live there. The dwelling-house of that time was on a level with the mill and attached to it, and must have been hundreds of years old. A new house a little removed from the mill was soon afterwards built, but I think I might safely say that that old house and the mill were at that time amongst the oldest buildings in the parish or in the surrounding parishes, excepting only the parish churches, and the most ancient portions of Amroth Castle.

My recollection of this old house is as follows, but perhaps something should be allowed for the long lapse of time since I saw it, and the exaggerated ideas formed in the mind of a child; but in the main the picture is a true one. The house was entered from the end nearest the mill, between it and which there was a narrow gangway occupied by rough stone steps leading externally from the level of the lower to that of the upper floor of the mill; both the mill and the house being built against the foot of a hill, the earth at the back being level with the upper floor, facilitating the delivery of the unground corn to the top where it was wanted. On entering the house you found yourself in a pretty large room open to the smoke and soot begrimed rafters, and the black and rotten thatch covered with ancient dust and cobwebs, and having one of those large chimney corners within which the whole family could sit around the wood fire lit on the hearthstone, and which superior people now consider so picturesque, and which many prominent architects in these days imitate, but with the addition of much ornament and many comforts undreamt of in the old days.

At the farther end of this room there was a smaller room partitioned off which served as both parlour and bedroom for the master and mistress of the house, and a small portion of this second room was further partitioned to form a larder with a door from the large living-room or kitchen. Over these two small rooms there was in the roof space a 'towlad' or loft, giving about seven feet of headroom below it, and access to this loft was got by means of a ladder placed against the edge of the loft when in use, and which was pushed up to lie on the floor of the loft when not in use. It was up on this loft the children of the family mostly slept. Other members of the household would probably have a folding or cupboard bed in the living-room.

The ground floor was paved either with stone or mortar; the few windows were very small, and seldom made to open in these old houses, so that the fresh air and the healing and purifying rays of the sun were practically excluded from these dwellings. Many of them were built with one wall tight up against a bank or hill, as this one was, and all without any damp-proof coating to keep the moisture back, nor damp-course to prevent the moisture from rising from the foundations.

One morning, soon after we had gone to live at Garness Mill, my grandmother's sister, Aunt Betty, who for years lived with us, assisting my mother with her young and numerous family, was getting us children down from our 'towlad' bedroom. As she could not carry us down, she would go down the ladder backwards, and we in turn would immediately follow her, she in the meanwhile carefully guarding us lest we should fall, and at the same time with one hand guiding our feet one after the other on to the rounds *(rungs)* of the ladder. I was a heavy, fat child, and naturally at four and a half years of age my legs were not very long. She found it difficult to make my legs stretch from one round to the next, so she exclaimed, "Why, Ben, boy, th' legs be too short to come down the ladder. Tha' must go to William Allen and have 'em made longer".

Now William Allen, as everybody knows, was the blacksmith of Milton and his smithy at that time was only two small meadows away from the Mill, and I had soon found this wonderful place out, and had made the acquaintance of the smith - the "mighty man" with "large and sinewy hands" whose hair was "crisp, and black, and long", and who was in every other respect true to the description of the village blacksmith by Longfellow. I also loved

"to see the flaming forge
And hear the bellows roar,
And watch the burning sparks that flew
Like chaff from the threshing floor".

But I had also seen how William Allen could make a short, thick piece of iron into a long thin one, and it is quite certain Aunt Betty had also seen, and her hint was sufficient to get my reasoning faculties at work: if he could lengthen a piece of iron, why shouldn't he lengthen my legs?

I was so taken by the idea that I must have got over my breakfast very expeditiously, and hurried with all possible speed across the little meadows and over the stile at the end of them to the smithy at Milton, for I found when I got there that William Allen was still at his breakfast. I went into the house close by where he lived, and found him and his wife Fanny, and, I believe, some of their children having their food at a round table in the part of the room near the door where I entered, and at the farther side of the room sat his father, old Billy Allen, who was a blacksmith likewise, and his wife, also having their breakfast. "Well, Ben, what dost *thee* want," said William. I boldly and in all seriousness explained to him the nature of my errand, and he as seriously, and, I thought, sternly listened to and considered the practicability of my proposal (at the same time he must have been almost bursting with laughter).

After, apparently, well weighing the question in his mind, he said to me, "Well, boy, if I am to make th' legs longer, I must cut 'em off first," probably thinking that the prospect would drive the idea out of my mind; but it didn't. It depressed me, but I still held on. The old man, looking at me through his spectacles from the other side of the room, took pity on me and said, "Don't thee harken to old William. Come thee over here by me. I'll take care of thee, and we'll make th' legs longer without cutting them off".

Thus comforted and encouraged, I crossed over, and stood by the kind old man's knee until breakfast was over, when I accompanied the two smiths to the smithy across the way. How long I remained there I cannot now say, but I doubtless wore out William Allen's patience at last, and I have no doubt it took him some time to hit upon a means of teaching me a lesson, and at the same time to accomplish the end I sought.

Now, William had a very surly-looking bull terrier dog named 'Pinchers', old and almost toothless, but artful and as knowing as his master. He was a terror to us children, for William had only to say in his gruff stern voice, "Pinchers, gripp'n!" and the ugly jaws would be about our ankles in a moment, holding us tightly, but at the same time careful not to hurt us. Old Pinchers was waddling about the workshop that day as usual, casting sidelong glances from bloodshot eyes about him, when suddenly his master called out, "Gripp'n, Pinchers!" I was out through the door like a shot from a gun, and up the road as fast as my short legs ever carried me, with the old dog making a big noise, and pretending to be very furious close at my heels. About 25 yards from the smithy there is a sharp bend in the road.

William followed us to the bend, and I can picture him now at that bend bursting with laughter, and I can hear him shouting after me, "That's the best way to make th' legs longer, boy"; and so it was.

Garness Mill in the 1850s

extracted from the Narberth Weekly News, October 11th 1923

Garness Mill! How the chatter of the little river (the 'lake' as it is called) comes back to me: the chuff-chuff-chuff from the water from the 'leat' as it filled the pockets of the dripping moss-grown wheel and sent it and the machinery of the mill merrily round, and the thundering roar of the water spout when it was turned off the wheel to form a foaming water-fall like an enormous white horse-tail twelve to fifteen feet in height; my father's excited rush to turn the water off when the corn ran out of the hopper sooner than he expected, and the whole concern seemed glad of the chance to run eagerly and madly to destruction!

What wonderfully busy days we occasionally had when a larger farmer would send his corn to be ground, perhaps several cartloads with strong men to carry the sacks of corn in, and the sacks of meal and flour out, and women to do the sifting when the meal came pouring down the spouts into the troughs! The, to us, mysterious bolter, which dealt with the ground wheat and separated it into several grades of 'superfine', 'fine', 'coarse', etc., down to the final 'bran', all of which it delivered automatically from its several spouts into sacks tied up to the nozzles! My father, with his clothes and hair and whiskers all powdered white with fine meal flying about, full of responsibility and watchfulness; and my mother at her best preparing the food for these infrequent visitors, when the best china and other utensils would be called into use.

These were days of great excitement - red-letter days. I regret to think that these old mills are fast falling out of use in these days, and with them the old customs connected with them. The smaller farmers would have their corn ground a little at a time, and would often get the miller to send his boy to fetch it and take it back in sacks thrown across the backs of donkeys. The pay for this and the grinding would be a certain measure of corn, which the miller would take for every bushel brought to be ground, and I think it was sometimes hinted that he seldom forgot to take his full quantity.

I have often tried to get at the derivation of the name 'Garness'. The first syllable is doubtless from the Welsh *Carn*, a heap of stones, and there are plenty of stones there to justify the word, but I cannot fit in the termination 'ess'. 'Carnedd', I could understand; perhaps someone will be so good as to help me in regard to Carn*ess* or Y Garness, which doubtless was the ancient form.

(In fact the name is first recorded in 1712 as the Gardenes, while Garness Mill appears as Gardeners Mill in 1723. The modern form seems to be a corrupted development - editor.)

I will not try to mention all the new experiences which came into my life on going to the old mill to live; things that fixed themselves indelibly in my young mind, not to be forgotten so long as I have breath. Amongst other things, I recall that my brother Tom and I seem to have spent weeks catching trout and eels in the partly dry bed of the 'leat' when father had turned the water off to do some necessary repairs to the artificial water course. I have a mental picture of the bank glistening with the writhing, speckled and silvery fish, and we both without a dry rag upon our bodies.

By the way, this word 'leat', although a perfectly appropriate English word, is seldom or never used in England. I have tried in many parts, but have always found a complete ignorance of its meaning or use. This remark applies to many old words and old forms of words in constant use in Pembrokeshire, but completely forgotten in England. It would be interesting to have a list of these, as well as of words adopted from the Welsh, such as 'Glastir', *(Glas ddwr)*, 'Doibil', 'Bach', etc.

A Portrait of Lanteague: Church and Mountain in the 1860s

extracted from the Narberth Weekly News, April 19th 1923

The church is a grey edifice of ample size for the population, with a square tower - all of considerable antiquity. I have never learnt when it was built or by whom, nor to whom it is dedicated. It stands in its little 'God's Acre' (the only burying place in the parish down to within living memory) by itself in the middle of the fields, a quarter of a mile or more from the village, and out of sight from there, and one cannot help wondering why on earth a church should be built in such an isolated position. There is a delightful old lane leading from the village to and past the church, or within about 100 yards of it, and I have a vivid recollection of going along it in the very early 'sixties' *(1860s)* on a bright spring or early summer Sunday morning. I fancy even now I can smell the sweet-scented hawthorn and new-mown hay in my nostrils, and see the men in their white or yellow corduroy trousers or breeches, grey or brown homespun coats, low-crowned beaver hats, and heavy, well-cleaned and greased hob-nailed boots, and the younger women and girls in peaked bonnets and lilac gowns, well flounced and expanded with crinolines, with perhaps a light shawl thrown over their shoulders, and a great display of wide ribbon fastening the bonnet, and tied in large bows under the chin, as we all went to or came from church, where the good and highly respected Parson Phillips conducted the service in simple but very effective style, assisted by his clerk, Old Billy Allen, the blacksmith of Milton, who was then a very aged man, and whose voice trembled very markedly as he gave the responses, or 'pitched' the tunes.

Lanteague Mountain, which was a 'mountain' only in the local use of the word, a piece of rough land which had not been cultivated, was then a common, said to be a mile each way, but was really considerably less. It was covered by a very poor kind of furze, ferns, and heather, with a little grass of poor growth in between. All those living around could turn their cattle on to it to pick up what they could, and most of the poorer people had a cow and heifer, a donkey, or perhaps two, geese, ducks, fowls, or perhaps a pony or a few sheep, searching for a very lean living on this bleak and miserable common. Poor as it was, it was a decided help to the poor people; but somewhere between '60 and '64 I remember seeing men with rods and chains, and, I presume, theodolite, measuring and surveying the 'Mountain', and some sort of arrangement was subsequently made, probably under the Commons Enclosure Act *(Enclosure Award, 1868)* by which it was divided and allocated to different persons, so that it has now long been private property, and several good houses have been built upon it with more or less ground attached.

The only industry, apart from agriculture, within the parish was the limestone quarries, and lime-burning at Trenewydd. There was no public-house in the parish, nor nearer than the Roses, Tavernspite, the Commercial Inn *(near Kilanow Cross, now a private house)*, or Amroth, and I never heard of any serious crime nor of anyone being sent to prison from there. Although I often heard threats of having someone up 'before his betters', or before 'Awd Bugby' *(the local magistrate)*.

FAVOURITE NAMES

A survey of Victorian forenames in Crunwere, by Judith Lloyd

What's in a name? Actually quite a lot. Examination of the population censuses for Crunwere, taken every ten years between 1841 and 1891, reveals a definite pattern of favourite Christian names in the parish.

In 1841 the most popular names here for girls were Elizabeth (31 examples found in the census), Mary (22), Sarah (19), Anne/Ann (18) and Jane (15). This accords with the Indexes of Births for England and Wales in 1838, showing Mary, Sarah, Elizabeth, Anne and Jane (in that order) as the most common forenames. In Crunwere there was also a liking for Martha (10) and Margaret (7), while Theodosia (2) and Rebecca (2) harked back to pre-Victorian favourites.

Similarly, the most popular names nationwide for boys in 1838 were William, John, Thomas, George and James; and in the Crunwere census for 1841 we find John (28), William (26), and Thomas (13), although only seven males named James and just three named George. Locally popular were Benjamin (7), Richard (7) and David (4), and reflecting Biblical tastes, one example each of Abraham, Shem, Lot, Titus and Theophilus.

In the 1851 census, Elizabeth (30), Anne/Ann (27) and Mary (26) were still the favoured names for females, with Sarah (17) and Jane (11) runners-up. Margaret was not far behind (9) together with Martha (7) and Theodosia (4). There were also three examples of Jennet, probably a diminutive form of Jane. The forenames for males still showed John the most popular (29), followed by William (25) and Thomas (15), with Benjamin and David (7 each), James (6), Richard (5) and Robert (4) trailing. We also see Welsh names making an appearance in this census - Griffith (3), Lewis (3), and Howell (1) - and a single rather German-looking Lodwig.

Ten years later, in 1861, the basic stock of forenames had grown considerably, possibly reflecting greater literacy and better communication in the area. Sharing the national pattern for girls' names, Elizabeth (24), Mary (16) and Sarah (11) remained at the top of the list here in Crunwere, with Anne/Ann (11), Martha (10), Margaret and Jane (9). Theodosia and Rebecca were still in the census; but these traditional old names were being overtaken by the more recently fashionable Mary Ann (4), Mary Ellen (1) and Ada (3), together with single examples of Caroline, Catherine, Cecilia, Hannah, Harriet, Esther, Frances, Jessie and Phoebe.

Boys' names appeared slower to change from the traditional stock in this census, with John and William neck and neck (26), followed by Thomas (10) and David and James (8 each). Robert (6) and Benjamin (5) were also still popular; as were the Welsh names Griffith, Howell and Lewis; but the more up-and-coming names are represented by examples of Allen,

Alfred, Leslie, Lionel, Stephen and Derrick.

The 1871 Crunwere census is the only one in which the spelling of forenames was not standardised, and most probably reflects the pronunciation of the day. Thus we find Theodoshia (1) and Pheby (1) with Jenate (2) and Cathrin (3), Charlette (1) and Susania (1). Elizabeth was still far and away the most popular of the girls' names (17), followed by Mary (13), Jane (9), Sarah and Anne/Ann (8 each), with Margret (7) just behind. Among the newcomers were Sarah Ann and Sarah Jane.

The spelling of boys' names in this 1871 census likewise displays a charming originality, with examples of Alphreat (2), Josheph (2), Benjamain (3) and Mikel (1). William (22) and John (20) still headed the list in popularity, followed by Thomas (8) and David (6).

The Indexes of Births for England and Wales in 1875 show Mary, Elizabeth and Sarah holding their place as the top three most popular names for girls. The Crunwere parish census for 1881 reflects this, with Elizabeth (17) and Mary (13) followed by Ann/Anne/Annie (9), Sarah (8) and Jane (8). We also find one example each of the more modern Susan, Penelope and Emma, along with Fannie and Minnie.

Countrywide, William, John and George were the top three for 1875. Here in Crunwere in 1881, it was still John (22) and William (20) the most favoured, with George way down the list (3). Thomas was holding in popularity (8) as was Benjamin/Ben (5) followed by the small group of Welsh forenames - Griffith (2), Howell (2), Lloyd, Owen and Evan (1 each). Arthur was a newcomer in this census, as was Peter and Talbot.

The final census of the 19th century, that of 1891, shows very little change in the overall popularity of traditional forenames in the parish. There are single instances of Gwendoline, Betsy and Lucy to add a modern flavour to the list, but overall the old stock still endured, with Elizabeth and Mary (both 14) still ahead of Anne/Ann (9) and Sarah (8). Jennet reappeared in the guise of Jannette, but Theodosia and Rebecca had disappeared entirely.

It was a similar pattern locally for boys' names. William (18) and John (15) were still the most popular in Crunwere, heading the traditional stock which included James and Thomas (7 each) and even Benjamin - hanging on with a solitary example. (There were also isolated recordings throughout all six censuses of Joseph, Charles, Daniel and Henry, clearly never great favourites here.) But from 1891 the trend was now towards the more recognisably 20th century names - Albert, Cecil, Frank, Godfrey and

Ivor, all with one example each - which were to become more prevalent by the close of the Edwardian era.

THE POOR HOUSE

Poorhouses (almshouses), were used in many parishes to house paupers who were chargeable to the parish. The Poor Law Amendment Act of 1835 introduced the setting up of 'Unions', each having a Workhouse and a Board of Guardians. There were 52 parishes in the Narberth Union, and each one would send their poor to the Workhouse at Union Hill, Narberth (*built in 1839 and now called Allensbank*), instead of caring for them in their own parish as they had previously done. Rates were levied in all the parishes for this purpose.

Letters in Haverfordwest Record Office dated 10th and 25th March 1857 give us the following information on the old Poor House in Llanteg:

The writer had been to Lanteague *(sic)* and said that it was unanimously agreed that the house had been built between 40 to 45 years ago and that it was nearly 30 years ago since the last piece of ground was enclosed. "John Morgan says he has been here 22 years, and there have been no additions made to it since he came - both Morgan and the Llanteague Party (*Poor Law Board?*) suppose it to have taken place in Mr Griffiths's time". It is said to have been in a sad, dilapidated state, the roof being "half off the House now and half the front wall down".

As an aside, the writer, Mr C. Griffiths, states that there had been about 16 inches of snow on the land around Llanteague (25th March).

The Poor Law Board were applying to the Rev. J. H. A. Philipps, M.A., Vicar of Madeley, as 'Lord of the Manor', for the sanction to sell and asking whether he had any claim in respect of the property. It was described as a freehold cottage by the name of 'Poor House', with a garden behind and another small garden in front. Also a small field which together with the site of the house and gardens extended to 1 acre, 1 rood and 15 perches of land.

The Poor Houses were shown in the following census returns:-

1841 - two properties mentioned: one with Lewis and Sarah Harry (aged 89 and 70 years); the other with Lewis and Elizabeth David (both aged 85) and Sarah Lewis (aged 65).

1851 - two properties mentioned: one occupied by John and Sarah Rees (aged 37 and 39) with their family of five children, mother-in-law and

nephew; the other with David and Elizabeth Davies (aged 44 and 46) with their five children and a nursling, William Webb.
(*We have been unable to find locations of these properties; but interestingly, in both the 1841 and 1851 censuses the John Morgan referred to in the letter above was residing at Middleton.*)

LIFE IN THE MID 19TH CENTURY

Until fairly recently rural parishes in Wales, as elsewhere, were largely self-sufficient and only on rare occasions did people find it necessary to venture far outside their community in search of a livelihood. Most inhabitants were born, lived and died within their own communities, to which they were bound by ties of blood and neighbourliness.

As a result of the decline of rural industry we have lost something very special. The social importance of the small craft workshops as meeting places for villagers cannot be overestimated. In many cases the smithy and the carpenter's yard were social centres where news and problems were discussed.

Life and Traditions in Rural Wales 1976

The census for Crunwere in 1851 shows the variety of occupations of those living in the parish, excluding farmers, agricultural labourers and domestic servants.

Registrar of births etc., lime merchant	R.W.W.Morgan, Trenewydd
Mason	Joseph Waters, Three Wells
Mason	Griffith Wilkins, The Den
Cooper	John Phillips, Furzy Park
Mason	William James, Brimy Lake
Land Proprietor	Ann McIntyre, Brimy Lake
Stonemason	Thomas Thomas, Rhydgoch
Rector	W. D. Phillips, Rectory
Gardener	John Jenkins, Lanteague
Carpenter	William Jenkins, Lanteague
Butcher	Allen Palmer, Golden Lion (*Laurels*)
Clockmaker	John Risley, Golden Lion (lodger)
Toll Collector/Schoolmaster	William Oriel, Tollgate
Carpenter	William Oriel, Milton Back

Carpenter	John James, Milton
Carpenter	William James, Milton
Blacksmith	William Allen senior, Milton
Blacksmith	William Allen junior, Milton
Miller	Rebecca Oriel, Garness Mill
Shopkeeper	Ann Kendrick, Moors
Carpenter	Thomas Oriel, Moors
Broom-maker	John Rees, Poorhouse
Shopkeeper	David Lewis, Ruelwall
Blacksmith	Daniel Griffiths, Crafty
Fishmonger	John Morgan, Middleton
Carpenter	Thomas Hodge, Bellevue
Carpenter	John Hodge, Bellevue
Land Proprietor	William Thomas, The Griggs
Tailor	William Griffiths, The Lodge
Seamstress	Elizabeth Griffiths, The Lodge
Seamstress	Mary Griffiths, The Lodge
Tailor	John Griffiths, The Lodge

OAKLANDS

parish of Crunwere, Llanteg

by Judith Lloyd

Oaklands House with Roy James, c.1952

Photo: Audrey James

The house may stand on earlier foundations, but in its present form dates from the early 1830s when the new turnpike road was built to the south of Crunwere Church. Originally two rooms deep and three storeys high, it was an inn or posting station named The Royal Oak, with stables and quarters to the rear. Beer was brewed in a malthouse at the foot of the large chimney: the kiln could still be seen as late as the 1940s. The first building on the site may well have been built down in the valley of a stream (which still flows in wet winters) because the turnpike road runs past it along the top of a short embankment. The 1841 census *(below)* describes the property as one building at this time, suggesting the adjoining house (no.2, the farmhouse) was added later. On the 1843 Ordnance Survey map it is shown as The Royal Oak. After becoming a farm apparently around the late 1840s, the name was altered to (the) Oakland, and a little later, Oaklands. In 1841 the landowner was John Henry Phillips, whose estate also included Folly Cross, Trenewydd, Trenewydd Lodge, Ruel Wall, Blackheath, and the Vicarage *(not the Rectory, which was a separate property).*

Crunwere census of 1841

The Royal Oak

	Jane Griffiths, 16 (?)	publican
	Anne Thomas, 19	female servant
	Elizabeth Eynon, 16	female servant
stables		
	Phillip Evans, 35	manservant
	William Richard, 23	manservant

Parish of Crunwere, 1842

Rent charges in lieu of tithes payable to the Rector:

landowner John Henry Phillips

occupier Thomas Voyle

lands (16 acres) and premises:

Oak Mountain, pasture	2/8
Oak Mountain, arable	2/1
Furzy Hill, pasture	6d
Lower Mountain, pasture	9d
The Royal Oak inn	1/7

Crunwere Census of 1851 (night of 30th March)

Shown for Oakland *(sic)*

Elizabeth Morgan, aged 66, widow, annuitant occupying 40 acres. Born Cheriton, Pembs.

Elizabeth Morgan, her daughter, aged 36, unmarried annuitant. Born Crunwere.

Thomas Voyle, her brother, aged 64, agricultural labourer, formerly tanner. Born Cheriton.

Ann James, servant, aged 24, housemaid. Born Crunwere.

James Davies, servant, aged 15. Born Eglwyscymmin.

The census states that one house at Oaklands is uninhabited, so by this time the adjoining farmhouse property - no.2 - had been built on to the eastern side of the existing building. Interestingly, there are two connecting passages, now bricked up, between the houses, so it must have been at this period that the old inn was extended at the rear. Elizabeth Morgan, given as head of the household in this census, was the widow of Robert Morgan (see below) who had previously farmed Trenewydd. She died in 1855, eight years after her husband. Their son, Robert W.W.Morgan, appears in this 1851 census as a bachelor of 26 living at Trenewydd, being described as Registrar of Births and Deaths, lime merchant, and farmer of 480 acres. It is possible his father was forced through ill health to give up Trenewydd to his son and semi-retire to farm the smaller holding at Oaklands.

Tombs in Crunwere churchyard

1. Robert Morgan of Oakland *(sic)* and late of Trenewydd
d. Dec 27th 1847 aet 65
and wife Elizabeth d. 1855
and fourth daughter Ann d. 1826 aet 8
and third daughter Elizabeth d. Jan 11th 1860 aet 44
Rev. Richard Morgan, eldest son,
Vicar of Aberavon and Bagland *(sic)*
d. March 9th 1851 aet 42

2. Cecil Lewis, of Oaklands
d. Mar 3rd 1863 aet 67

Rev. Richard Morgan (above) lived at Heatherland. The east window of Crunwere Church was given by his widow in his memory. This widow was Georgiana Morgan (see note below for Heatherland), their daughters being Catherine and Emma.

Crunwere Census of 1861

Everyone appears to have been absent from Oaklands on the night the census was taken, because the only names under the entry are:

Jane James, aged 21, spinster; house servant, born Crunwere.
Richard Thomas, aged 15, farm servant, born Laugharne.

These two servants are very probably the individuals mentioned by Ben Price in his childhood reminiscences in a newspaper article in 1924 where he refers to a servant named Dick at Oaklands and one housemaid, both employed by Miss Jane Morgan 'the daughter of Trenewydd', who ran a singing school for local children in her kitchen.

John Higgon

A conveyance dated 1867 between him and landowner John Arthur Philipps Scourfield is among the house deeds. He may have been of the same family as a Mr Higgon who owned New House and Welsh Furze at Princes Gate from 1770.

Crunwere Census of 1871

Shown under entry for Oaklands:

Jane Morgans *(sic)* , head of the household, spinster aged 48, farming 50 acres; born Crunwere
Hughs, Georgiana, her niece, spinster aged 21, visitor
Elizabeth Morgan, aged 21, general and domestic servant
Thomas Morgan, aged 27, farm servant

Crunwere Census of 1881

Shown under the entry for Oaklands:

Lloyd Rice Philipps, aged 54, farmer of 50 acres employing labourer. Born Abergwili, Carmarthenshire.
Maria Ann, his wife, aged 54. Born Abergwili *(cf 1891 census).*
Georgiana Maria, his daughter, aged 22. Born East Indies.
John George, his son, aged 13, scholar. Born Lampeter Velfrey.
Jane Morgan, aged 58. Annuitant. Born Crunwere.
Thomas Morgan, her brother, aged 70. Born Henrys Moat.
Emma J.Morgan, her niece, aged 34. Born Aberavon, Glamorgan.
Mary Davies, domestic servant, aged 20. Born St. Issels.

The same census shows that Heatherland was occupied by Georgiana Catherine Morgan, aged 60, a lady of private income, born Abergwili, and her unmarried daughter Catherine Morgan, aged 30, born Aberavon. It seems highly probable that Georgiana Morgan was the sister of Maria

Philipps and a relation by marriage to Jane Morgan, and that Emma J.Morgan (above) was Catherine Morgan's sister, implying that the two families occupying Oaklands and Heatherland at this time were closely interrelated.

Jane Morgan is buried in Crunwere churchyard. Her tombstone describes her as born April 26th 1822, dying May 4th 1884. Georgiana Morgan died on May 22nd 1897 at Heyope Rectory, Knighton, Radnorshire, and is buried beside Jane Morgan.

Lloyd Philipps was descended from the two ancient and distinguished Carmarthen families of Philipps and Rice. Earlier in his career he had been a Captain in the 33rd Madras Infantry, India, where two of his older children, Georgiana and Herbert, were born. He was buried in Crunwere churchyard on April 27th 1908, aged 82 years, just nine days after the interment of his wife Maria Ann, also aged 82 years.

1884 Abstract of Lease (Haverfordwest Record Office)

Several pieces or closes of land commonly called or known by the name of Trenewydd Lands or Trenewydd South Lands containing by estimate 133 acres, 2 rods and 16 perches or thereabouts, being part of Trenewydd Farm formerly held by Henry Owen Makin Esq., and having the northern boundary of the southern hedge of the field called the Welshman's Mountain, the western hedge of the Vineyard field, the southern hedge of the Lodge Cottage garden, the southern hedge of Ash Longlands, from thence diverging across part of the Ash Longlands in a straight line through the Eastern Mountain to the southern hedge of the Brake Park and along the same, then down the western hedge of the Crafty Park to the northern hedge of the New Road using Llanteg Mountain as the eastern boundary, the lands of Miss Philipps and of John Philipps Esq. of Pendeilo as the southern boundary and the farms of Horsemantown *(sic)* and Gellyhalog as the western boundary of the same, and also all that messuage or dwelling house commonly called the Royal Oak with the outbuildings and buildings belonging to Robert Morgan and seasonally all that field of land part of the Brake Park containing 6 acres.

(Formerly in the occupation of Elizabeth and Jane Morgan together with all buildings and common of pasture on Llanteg Common. They undertook not to plough up or convert to tillage more than half the arable lands demised, and not to carry away grass but to convert to manure on the premises. Elizabeth and Jane Morgan were also permitted to dig limestone

in the quarries.)
Crunwere Census of 1891
Shown under the entry for Oaklands:

Lloyd R.Philipps, aged 64, living on own means. Born Abergwilly *(sic)*

Maria, his wife, aged 64. Born St Peters, Carmarthen *(cf 1881 census)*

John, his son, aged 23, student of theology. Born Lampeter Velfrey

Godfrey Darbertt (?) his grandson, aged 8 (?). Born Bramley, Surrey

William Davies, aged 61, Congregational minister and farmer. Born Llanboidy

Sarah, his wife, aged 60. Born St Peters, Carmarthen

William, his son, aged 24, 'farmer's son'. Born Lawrenny

Anne, his daughter, aged 26. Born Lawrenny

Sarah, his daughter, aged 21. Born Lawrenny

William Davies senior was gored to death by a bull in the fields behind Oaklands. He is buried in the Congregational Chapel yard together with other members of the family. The tombstone - an obelisk - describes him as serving as a minister for over forty years and gives his dates as Sept 20 1828 - May 20 1902. His wife Sarah's dates are April 14 1830 - August 23 1904. His daughter Anne (A.M.) died in 1894 aged 29; and his daughter Sarah (S.J.), was born on March 16 1870, dying on March 17 1892, aged exactly 22 years and one day.

This 1891 census also shows Heatherland still occupied by Georgiana C.Morgan, aged 70, widow, born Cwmgwilly, 'living on her own means'; her daughter Catherine, aged 36, also living on her own means; her nephew, Herbert S.Philipps (son of Lloyd, Oaklands) aged 28, described as steward (presumably of her estate), whose birthplace was Madras; and her grandson Ivor Evans, aged 5 months(?) born at Fenton in Staffordshire.

Were Sarah Davies and Maria Philipps sisters, both being born in St Peters (if this census is correct and the one for 1881 giving Maria's birthplace wrongly - Abergwili and St Peters, Carmarthen, are neighbouring parishes). If so, Sarah Davies was probably also the sister of Georgiana Morgan of Heatherland. Coincidentally, this same census shows a Mrs

Henrietta E.Phillips living 'on her own means' at Crunwere Rectory. She is described as mother-in-law of the rector William Garner, her age given as 73, and her birthplace as St Peters, Carmarthen. Was she another of the Heatherland/Oaklands connection?

Crunwere Tax Book 1911

The 'owner of the building' is given as Jane Lewis; while the house occupant is Georgiana Philipps. Sir O.Scourfield is the landowner.

A few days before Christmas the same year (1911) a 31 year old merchant seaman named George Thomas Welsh died at Oaklands of tuberculosis and exhaustion. Georgiana Philipps was present at his death and registered it with the authorities, which suggests that he may have been lodging at the house.

As late as the 1940s there was still no piped water at the property. Despite the existence of three wells (one, called the winch, immediately to the north-west corner of the house, another a few yards to the east, and a third across the road where there was a small orchard) water was fetched from Castle Ely and stored in a tank by the back door.

Extract from house deeds

In 1923 Oaklands Farm, comprising buildings and land of 53 acres, and owned by Henry Gwyn Davies Scourfield (formerly Henry Gwyn Saunders Davies), was sold to Thomas Evan Lewis, for £1,275. (The latter continued to own the land and 2 Oaklands until his death in 1940.) At this period - 1923 - the trustees of the estate were William Lea, Ethelbert Edward Lort Philipps, and Arthur Owen Saunders Davies. In the same year, 1 Oaklands was sold separately to Miss Marion Powell for £150. The Powells came from St Tydfil's, Merthyr Vale. On Marion Powell's death in 1938 the property passed to her sisters, Annie (d. 1944) and Josephine (d. 1946). Their testator was a Rev. Thomas Evans, who in 1947 sold the house to Mari Gwendolen Bennett, of Myrtle Grove, Patching, Sussex, for £300. Mrs Bennett was a relative of Georgiana Philipps *(see above)* who throughout this time was occupying 1 Oaklands (now Oaklands House), continuing to do so until her death in 1948.

EXTRACTS FROM THE PARISH MAGAZINE - 1897

May - in the March 29th meeting Messrs J.Allen, Milton Back, and T.Phillips, Middleton were appointed overseers for the coming year.

July - on the 22nd, 132 parishioners went to the Rectory in respect of invitations sent out, the children had tea and cake and the adults cold beef etc. Then to a neighbouring field where sports were played for several hours. An exhibition of musical drill was given by the schoolchildren - presents of sweets, biscuits, toys etc. were distributed. The event ended with a vote of thanks, cheers for the Queen and the singing of the National Anthem.

9 September - two serious accidents were recorded:-

William James, Broomylake, while repairing an outhouse, slipped off the ladder and received internal injuries. He died on the 15th.

John Price, a servant in the employment of William John, was severely kicked by a horse belonging to a neighbour. He is now recovering.

CRUNWERE BURIALS 1813-1920

During these 107 years there were 396 burials at Crunwere Church, averaging between three and four a year. 1853 stands out as a particularly bad year as there were thirteen burials. 1917/18/19 do not show a high degree of deaths so Crunwere must have escaped the worst ravages of the Spanish 'Flu epidemic, except for Mrs Charlotte Dunbar, Headmistress, who died of the influenza in December 1918.

Personal tragedies are revealed with the burials of three people from the Folly between the 10th and 27th of January 1815 (William aged 22, Hannah aged 21, and baby John 11 months).

Childhood mortality again affected one household in 1894 when two children from Crafty, Agnes May and Florence Phillips, were buried between the 15th and 28th May aged just 1 year and 4 years old.

The oldest person to be buried was Martha Thomas of Summerhill who was 102 years when she died in February 1822. Mary Price of Lanteague is recorded as being 101 years when she died in 1893, and Elizabeth Davis of Bevlin 100 years when she was buried in 1849. In contrast the youngest burial was in February 1910 when baby Agnes John of Llanteg Farm died aged just six and a half hours.

Thomas Oriel, who died in 1848 aged four months, was living on Caldey Island; while Thomas James from Milton died in London aged 26 years in 1858.

Some people who are buried in Crunwere churchyard must have had rather grim ends to their lives, dying in the Narberth Union Workhouse *(now Allensbank)*.

They are recorded as:

James Dalton, aged 92, died 1863.
John Hodge, aged 14 months, died 1881.
Mary Griffiths, aged 85, died 1898.
Celia Dalton, aged 65, died 1899.
Mary Wilkins, aged 78, died 1910.

Another poor unfortunate was George Lewis, who died in 1904 aged 61 years at the Lunatic Asylum at Carmarthen.

Breakdown of Burials 1813-1920

Age	Burials
0-2	65
3-9	30
10-19	31
20-39	53
40-59	47
60-79	101
80-99	66
100+	3

JOHN AND ELIZABETH (BETSY) THOMAS, GOLDEN LION

researched by Katherine Lloyd and Elizabeth and Michael Skinner

The photograph shows my great-grandparents, John and Elizabeth Thomas, who were married at Crunwere Church on January 23rd 1877. John was aged 52, a widower and servant of Trenewydd. His father Benjamin Thomas had been a labourer.

Elizabeth (known in the family as Betsy) was aged 39, a widow from Milton, whose father was John James, a labourer. The witnesses to the marriage were John Reynolds (possibly Betsy's son by her first marriage) and Anne James (her sister perhaps).

John and Betsy had one son, Benjamin (my grandfather) who was born at The Golden Lion, now known as The Laurels, on July 27th 1880. Benjamin was baptised at Crunwere Church on August 22nd 1880. (He became an engine driver on the Great Western Railways. Some readers may remember him and his wife Mabel and their children: Austin (my father), Gwen, Clarence and Vernon. The family lived in Whitland from 1919 until 1949 at St George's Cottage and Greylands.)

In the 1881 census, John (56) and Betsy (43) are listed as living at The Golden Lion with their son Benjamin (aged 8 months) and John's stepson George Reynolds (aged 9 years).

Ten years later, in the census of 1891, John (67) and Betsy (51) and their son Benjamin (10) are still living at The Golden Lion. By then George Reynolds had left home.

The Golden Lion was originally an inn, and appears as such in the 1841 census, the landlord being Allen Palmer living with his wife Martha. The inn closed sometime between 1841 and 1851, because although Allen Palmer was still there, he was by now trading as a butcher not a publican. We believe that sometime between 1891 and 1918 The Golden Lion was renamed The Laurels, and this is what it is known as today.

At sometime after 1891 John and Betsy moved to a cottage at Amroth, on the Amroth Castle estate. We have a copy of a document relating to the sale of the estate dated July 20th 1898, in which the cottage is clearly named Amroth Castle Arms - having once been an inn, we suspect. In 1898 the property consisted of two cottages with gardens covering an area of 3 roods, 23 perches, and held 'with other property by Mr Thomas' at an annual rent of £6 10s (though whether this was our John Thomas we are not sure). The cottage no longer exists, but is now a small car park opposite the entrance to Amroth Castle. There is what we believe to be the remains of a drift mineshaft at the rear of the property, which was never worked but abandoned in 1820.

John Thomas died on December 2nd 1910, aged 86. His death

certificate gives his address as Beach Cottage, Amroth. We do not know the precise location of this property, nor do we know the relationship of Thomas John (who was present at the death) to my great-grandfather. John Thomas is buried at Amroth Parish Church, on his own.

John Thomas

John started his life at Trelissy, the first son of Benjamin and Sarah Thomas (nee John), who were married at Crunwere Parish Church on November 1st 1823 by Thomas Dalton, the Rector at that time. Benjamin signed his name, but Sarah could not write. The marriage took place 'with consent of parents'.

John and his sister Mary were both baptised at Amroth Church, the nearest church to Trelissy. John was baptised on February 15th 1824, and Mary on 22nd May 1825.

The family then moved to Folly, Llanteg. John's brother William and sister Sarah were baptised in St Elidyr's Church, Crunwere: William on September 17th 1826, and Sarah on December 2nd 1827.

In the 1841 census, Benjamin and Sarah are both aged 40, and living at Folly Cross with Sarah, their daughter aged 13. By that time John would have left home to work as a farm labourer, and we lose track of him, not finding him again until 1877 when he was a widower.

In the 1851 census John's sister Mary (aged 26) was then living at Folly with her parents.

Sadly, his sister Sarah died on July 25th 1856 aged only 28 years. Her grave is on the right hand side of the cobbled path at Crunwere Church, inscribed: 'In Memory of Sarah, daughter of Benjamin junior and Sarah Thomas of Folly in this Parish, who died July 25th 1856 aged 28 years - the Lord direct your harts into the love of God and into the patient (arms?) waiting for Christ'.

The various censuses show that Benjamin and Sarah lived at Folly for the rest of their lives. Benjamin died in 1868, but Sarah must have died after the 1871 census, because at that time she was living at the Folly on her own, aged 70.

Elizabeth (Betsy) Thomas

Elizabeth (Betsy) was born in Crunwere in May 1837, the daughter of John and Hester James. Little is known about her early years. We know that her first marriage was to William Reynolds, but she was widowed before the 1871 census, which shows her as Elizabeth Reynolds, widow aged 33, head of the household at Bountiland, with John her son (aged 11) and Ester her daughter (aged 9). Baby George was born later that year after his father William had died.

In 1889 Elizabeth's mother, Hester James, died aged 74, her address being The Golden Lion. This probably dated the family move from Crunwere to Amroth as being after 1889.

Older members of my family have always believed that Betsy was the unofficial midwife in Crunwere and Amroth. She helped to deliver many of those born in the area. It is said that when one of the chapels was being built in Crunwere, Betsy was asked to lay the corner stone. She must have felt very privileged to do this as she was Church, not Chapel.

Another family story is that when John and Betsy lived at Amroth they often helped out at Amroth Castle, especially when the owners were entertaining. Betsy's daughter-in-law, Mabel Rosina Thomas (my grandmother), carried a young baby girl from Amroth Castle to be christened at St Elidyr's Church, Amroth. That baby was the daughter of Lord and Lady Kylsant, who, many years later, became Mrs Fisher-Hoch of The Plas, Llanstephan. This would probably have been somewhere around 1908. After her husband's death in 1910, Betsy returned to Crunwere, strangely enough to the family home - The Laurels. She lived there with John and Elizabeth Raymond. John Raymond died in 1914 aged 78, and is buried at Crunwere Church. Elizabeth Raymond kept a grocer's shop, and later on the Post Office. I am sure that Betsy would have helped Mrs Raymond in the shop, despite her age; she would have enjoyed meeting people, many of whom she had helped bring into the world.

Betsy must have been a sprightly character. We have a cutting from a local paper in 1945 which related to her son Benjamin Thomas's retirement from the Great Western Railway. The article says "His mother, an accomplished step-dancer, attended the wedding *(in Merthyr Tydfil in 1907)* and performed her last step-dance twelve days before her 70th birthday".

Betsy ended her days, aged 82, in 1918 at The Laurels, where she must have spent many happy years. No doubt the village mourned her, for she must have been a very well-respected and popular lady. She is buried at Crunwere Church, possibly with her parents, or in an unmarked grave, for we have been unable to find her grave. Mrs Elizabeth Raymond died twenty years later, aged 89.

I am told that there is a family connection with the Raymonds, but have not fully researched it yet. My father's middle Christian name is Raymond, as is my brother's. The only connection that I have been able to make so far is that both the Raymonds and Betsy lived (and possibly worked) at Milton at one time. Betsy was there in 1877 as a widow aged 39, and John and Elizabeth Raymond were living there at the time of the 1871 census, John aged 25 and Elizabeth 23, with their daughter Margaret aged 8 months.

Were the Raymonds related to Betsy, or were they just good friends?

THE SCOURFIELD FAMILY OF LLANTEG

researched by Ian Smart

George and Susan Scourfield and their family lived in Llanteg during the early part of the 20th century and were committed worshippers at the Congregational chapel. Although they spent their last years in Whitland, they are both interred in the chapel burial ground in the neighbouring grave to one of their sons.

George was originally from Ludchurch, and he married Susan Phillips from Lampeter Velfrey in 1878. They first made their home in Susan's home village, but some time after 1891 they moved to Llanteg with their two sons and seven daughters. They lived in at least three different homes in Llanteg before retiring to Whitland in the 1930s.

Their children all married, but did not stay in Llanteg. Annie (b.1878) married Levee Jenkins and lived at Sardis. John (b.1880) was a quarryman who married Sally Phillips and lived in Cants together with their six children. Elizabeth (b.1883) married Harry Vincent and lived in Port Talbot, where their son still lives. Mary (b.1885) married Tom Lewis and at one point lived in Sutton Coldfield, although she died in Whitland. James (b.1886) died aged only 20 from meningitis, and is interred in the Congregational chapel burial ground. Susanna (b.1888) married Tom Roberts and moved to Whitland, where two of their daughters still live. Harriet (b.1891) married Willie James and lived in Carmarthen. Gladys (b.1898) married Alfred Harris and lived in Lampeter Velfrey. Cissie (b.1896) married Morgan Williams and they lived in Whitland with their seven children.

In Llanteg the Scourfield family lived in The Moors, The Griggs, and lastly Milton Back, which they left in 1934. George was an agricultural labourer, and a deacon at the Congregational chapel in the time of Rev. J.H.Phillips. This clergyman (who spent 23 years in Llanteg before moving to Tiers Cross) returned to preside at the funerals of George and Susan, indicating how highly he regarded their dedication to the chapel.

PART THREE

TWENTIETH CENTURY

PART THREE: TWENTIETH CENTURY

CRUNWERE CHURCH OF ENGLAND SCHOOL

Extracts from the Minute Book commenced 24 Sept 1904.

1906 - Summer Holidays fixed at four weeks from 16th July. School to re-open 13th August.

6 Apr 1906 - complaints had been received from some of the parents that their children had been roughly handled. It was decided that the Head Teacher (*Annie May Williams*) should be informed that where punishment was necessary, it should be inflicted with care.

1 July 1907 - Head Teacher has given three months notice (she stated that she was unable to find comfortable lodgings).

30 Sept 1907 - Miss Francis Edith Ellen Evans commenced duties as Head Teacher.

27 June 1908 - it was resolved that should the attendance fall off owing to the hay-making being in full swing, to close the school for the usual Summer Holiday.

7 Apr 1909 - the report of the Diocesan Inspector relating to the school was considered highly satisfactory. The General Report is as follows: "very good work has been done in this School and tone and discipline are excellent".

9 Feb 1910 - the school has been closed owing to so many children being laid up with bad colds, the Medical Officer of Health having given instructions to close the school for a fortnight.

9 Apr 1910 - it was unanimously decided to appeal to the Education Committee for an extra desk for the infants, there being only three desks for 22 children.

27 Apr 1910 - proposal carried that Mrs Emily Davies of Blackheath be appointed school cleaner.

23 Nov 1910 - carried unanimously that Mrs Dunbar be appointed Head Teacher.

15 June 1911 - at the request of the King unanimously carried that the children should have an extra week's holiday and that the summer holiday should immediately follow *(to celebrate the Coronation).*

18 Sept 1912 - the architect's plans for the extension of the school buildings were considered.

13 Mar 1913 - the Educational Medical Officer was closing the school on account of an outbreak of chicken-pox from Monday 10th March, and re-opening it on Tuesday 25th March.

15 Jan 1914 - the question of levelling the playground was discussed and it was decided to have the stones 'digged up', also that it should be covered with 'rab'. Mr Glanville kindly gave permission to get the 'rab' from Pensylvania (*the corner near the parish boundary*). He also undertook to drive some over, as did Mr Williams, Trenewydd, Mr J.Williams, Crunwere and Mr Davies, Greenacre.

6 Apr 1915 - the school cleaner, Mrs Emily Davies has sent in her resignation.

22 Sept 1916 - proposed and seconded that the children should have half a day's holiday on Empire Day.

8 July 1918 - proposed that Mr Abram Hodge be asked to give an estimate for ploughing the piece of ground required for a school garden.

Dec 1918 - owing to the death of Mrs Dunbar, a special meeting of the Managers was held. It was their desire to place on record their sense of the great loss the school had sustained by the death of the Head Teacher (*from influenza*) and also their high appreciation of the services so faithfully and successfully rendered by her during the eight years she was in charge of the school. The Correspondent was asked to convey to her children their deep sympathy with them in their bereavement. It was explained that the medical order closing the school extends from November 11th up to January 6th 1919 when the school will be re-opened in the charge of a temporary Head Teacher.

10 Apr 1919 - position regarding the school garden - only five children are at present of age to do gardening work and therefore only about one third of the area prepared can be cultivated this year.

31 Jan 1920 - concerning the objection made by the Board of Agriculture and Fisheries to the school garden in the Parish Recreation Ground (*now a small park area south of the old school house*), the managers were of the opinion that if the present garden cannot be retained, no other plot of ground for a garden convenient to the school is available.

28 Oct 1921 - the suggestion of the Head Teacher that a flower garden be made in the playground was agreed to.

9 Aug 1923 - meeting held to discuss the building of an additional bedroom to the School House. It was pointed out that it would be easily possible to put a third bedroom on top of the outer kitchen with the door to it at the top of the stairs; carried unanimously. It was considered that three tons of coal would be sufficient for the school winter supply.

27 Dec 1923 - the Managers decided to insure the piano for £50, the cost price.

31 Mar 1924 - the school would open during Summer Time from 9.30am to 4pm.

31 July 1925 - extract from letter by Mr E.T.Davies, Director of Education - "the committee approve of Mr F.E.C.Wolff as Head Teacher of Crunwere N.P. School. I have written asking him to commence duties on 7th Sept."

17 Feb 1926 - it was thought advisable that the repair of the footbridge near to the Cabin should be considered.

25 Feb 1926 - a Managers and Parish Council meeting was called to discuss the repairs and renewal of two footbridges, one near the Cabin, one near Milton Back. The footbridge near the Cabin is needed daily by school children. Attention was also drawn to the need of a rail near Lanteague Crossing (*Llanteg crossroads*) and the raising of the roadway a foot just beyond the crossing towards the school which after rain is 'overflooded'. Mr James, Clyngwyn, kindly undertook the repairs of the footbridge near the Cabin. Mr Williams, Whitland, was to have his attention drawn to the repairs needed to put the Milton Back footbridge safe.

4 Feb 1927 - there had been structural repairs made to the School House; the walls of the school ground repaired and 'jambs' built for the iron gate to the field, and for the door to the garden; a new range put in, and there was gravel for the yard. For several years the School House was unoccupied, the teacher taking rooms in the village and consequently no rent had been received. Paid £40 9s for mason work as above and £8 for carpenter's work, leaving about £50. This was considered a very satisfactory balance.

It was decided that a wooden shed, with a galvanised iron roof, sufficiently large to store benches and desks when not in use, as well as the 'platform' boards now stored in the Rectory barn, should be built to avoid the cartage after each entertainment held in the school.

The extension of the school room towards the entrance from the main road was discussed. This extension would soon be made compulsory owing to the increase in attendance of scholars. Mr A.James was to be asked to give measurements and an estimated cost. The work, when undertaken, was to be completed during the Summer Holidays (six weeks). Mr James was also to be asked to kindly give an estimate for an additional bedroom for the School House.

The Treasurer undertook to ascertain the amount of interest annually generated by the Merrilees Charity, and to find out to whom it had been paid in previous years and the amounts paid each year during the last ten years. (*Mr James Merrilees, a native of the Scottish lowlands, had lived at Stanwell Villa until his death in March 1896 at the age of 85.*)

24 Apr 1927 - the Treasurer received a letter from Barclays Bank. The 'Merrilees Charity', which represents 2s 3d quarterly, has accumulated to £1 11s 6d, which was held at the disposal of the Rector.

8 Nov 1927 - the Managers engaged a workman to tidy up the field used by the children as a playground; the hedges were trimmed, the briars cleared away and the field drain and ditch filled in.

11 Jan 1928 - a Valour gas stove was bought for the use of the school, to be near the door. A galvanised iron shed has been put up.

19 June 1928 - a meeting to arrange about the school children going by charabanc to the Missionary Exhibition at Tenby.

20 Jan 1930 - meeting to see about notices to be fixed up warning gypsies they were not to camp near the school.

21 Nov 1930 - presented the schoolchildren with a football.

Report of His Majesty's Inspectors (inspected 18th Nov 1929, 4th Nov 1931 and 10th May 1932):- "This is a small country school of 45 pupils and two teachers. Work is carried out in a crowded room. A low portable partition has recently been supplied to divide the two classes.

In the upper class the standard of work in the three 'R's' is poor. In arithmetic the children should work in well-defined groups according to their varying ability and close attention should be given to the marking of exercises. Adequate time should be given to mental arithmetic.

The pupils have some grasp of History, Geography and certain items of General Knowledge, due mainly to the Head Teacher's practice of reading to them from reference books and similar large volumes. It is very important that the other scholars be encouraged to read for themselves so that the Head Teacher's time can be devoted to the more backward scholars. Intense individual and group work is necessary to give the weaker children a chance of improvement. A little cardboard modelling is done and occasionally some fretwork. It is doubtful whether the fretwork has much educational value. Book binding would be a more suitable developement of the earlier work on cardboard".

5 Nov 1932 - discussed H.M.I. Report and considered the following suggestions:-

1) an additional room for infants.
2) enlargement of cloakrooms.
3) additional office (*lavatory*) for the girls.
4) re-gravelling the school yard.
5) repairs to the building.

20 Dec 1934 - the disposal of the Purser Fund *(a charity fund)* was discussed and finally decided that the money should not be given to the children this Christmas as in the past, but that it should be retained and utilised for taking the children for an educational tour during the summer months (36 seater bus £4 5s. May 15th, children and others to meet at school at 9.30am to visit St. David's).

1 May 1935 - Head Teacher's Report - he also complained of gypsies camping on the lane running alongside the school, leaving old tins and refuse about, and asked whether something could not be done to prevent them camping there.

23 Dec 1935 - in his report the Head Teacher pointed out that the number of scholars attending the school had dropped from 39 to 27.

Crunwere School 1930s **Photo: Connie Scourfield**

22 Apr 1936 - the children's educational trip will be via Llangwm, Rosemarket etc. to Milford Haven for lunch, returning to Haverfordwest for tea. It was decided that a sum not exceeding £5 be drawn from the school fund to augment the Purser Charity Fund. This sum to be repaid early in the autumn, the Head Teacher promising to get up a whist drive to do so. The trip was to be on 5th June. Leaving Llanteg Cross at 9.30am, The Folly 9.40am, Milford Haven 3.30pm (lunch at 1pm), and Haverfordwest at 8.30pm for home. The charge for outsiders to be 2/6 each with 1/- for lunch. Mr W.B.Davies proposed that a ready-cooked ham be bought and taken on the trip, together with bread, butter and tea.
8 June 1936 - much appreciation was expressed at the arrangements for the Children's Outing, but it was felt that the number which went for the trip was enormous and thus the trip had gone beyond what it was intended for at the start - viz. an educational tour for the children. It was proposed that in future all trips arranged for the children should be confined to the children, staff and any Manager with his wife who would care to join. Carried unanimously.
21 June 1937 - it was proposed that for this year the amount of money from the Purser Charity be divided equally among the scholars. In the Head Teacher's Report he stated that Master Noel Davies, Bryn Ely, had won a scholaship to Narberth County School at the early age of 10 years.
4 Oct 1937 - the Rector pointed out that during the following week (Tuesday 12th October), the new extension to the churchyard would be consecrated by the Lord Bishop of St. David's and that as the school room would be required for tea after the service he asked the Managers to allow a holiday for that day - granted.
27 Nov 1937 - the Rector gave the conditions governing the Purser Charity which is "that the sum of £100 in trust was left to the Rector of Crunwere (in perpetuity), the interest therein to be given annually to the most deserving in Crunwere School".
26 July 1938 - Rev. Morgan congratulated Mr Wolff the Head Teacher upon the good attendance attained during 1937, and also on the successes attained by the school at the sports held at Milford Haven on the previous Saturday.

A letter from the County Architect was then read out dealing with the playground, lavatories and drinking water. There was a unanimous decision that although the Managers were in full accord with the points raised, yet they did not feel justified in spending a large sum of money on improvements unless the Local Education Authority gave a guarantee that the school would not be closed for at least another seven years.

A water standard was to be erected in the very near future just outside the school premises.

(Crunwere School was built in 1876 and opened on 13th February 1877 with 15 pupils on the register. The School closed in December 1946.)

MEMORIES OF MY GRANDMOTHER - MRS CHARLOTTE DUNBAR, HEADMISTRESS of CRUNWERE SCHOOL 1910-1918

by Josephine Jenkins

Mrs. Charlotte Dunbar
Photo: Bernard Dunbar

One of the reasons why my grandmother Mrs Dunbar came to Crunwere in 1910 was to get away from the London smogs. She had thought that the clean air would be beneficial to her health.

By Christmas 1910, she had settled in Crunwere Schoolhouse with her two sons, Donald and Arthur.

It seems that she was a good teacher and also a strict disciplinarian, as the records show that the cane was in regular use, even for the girls!

My grandmother didn't appear to enjoy the good health that she had hoped for. The School Log Book confirms that she had regular absences due to illness.

During research into her life I was lucky enough to be put in touch in 1992 with a Mrs Eleanor Mary Phelps (nee Allen) who was nearly 90 years old. Mrs Phelps had been a pupil at Crunwere School when Mrs Dunbar had arrived. This lady was a joy to talk to and listen to and she had lots of memories of that time. One of the things she recalled was that she used to take books into the Schoolhouse to be marked by Mrs Dunbar when she lay ill in bed.

I suppose with her medical history my grandmother would have had little resistance to the Spanish 'Flu epidemic that swept the locality in 1918. On the 9th December of that year she died, aged 49 years.

The death of their mother must have been a devastating blow for her two sons. Not only did they lose their mother, they lost their only means of support and they also lost their home. In the aftermath of her death, *who* made the decisions that were to affect the rest of their lives and *why* those decisions were made are lost in the mists of time. Why two well-educated young men should have been regarded as only suitable for farm labouring, is one of the many unanswered questions. It must have been the bleakest time of their lives.

Arthur, aged 17 years, was away at college in 1918. He was not to return there. Instead, he found himself working on a local farm. The contrast between what had been his life just some eight years before when he had lived in London, and the manual graft of farm work, where he slept in a loft, probably shared with several others, can only be imagined. However at Trenewydd he was to find happiness. He met my mother, Winnie, who was in service there. They married at Crunwere Church in 1923, and moved to Whitland where they raised a large family. They shared more than 50 years of marriage. Arthur was a kind, good-natured father, who worked hard to provide for his family.

Arthur's brother Donald first went to work at Pontyberem, then returned to work on local farms, one of which was Eastlake. His last job was at Gellihalog Quarry where he built a wooden bungalow out of mahogany wood from a ship in Pembroke Dock (it is still there). At one time Donald played the organ at Crunwere Church. A crippling disease forced him to give up work at an early age. Donald then moved with his wife Jessie and their family to Temple Bar, Kilgetty, where he was looked after by them until his death in 1963.

My grandmother Charlotte's life was rarely talked about in our family home. My father never spoke about events at Crunwere, or his early life in London, and my mother also said very little. When I started searching I had nothing to go on. The school register for Crunwere gave me the previous school that Arthur and Donald had attended in London and I went from there. It has only added to the mystery surrounding my grandmother's life to discover that she had some independent means which enabled her to travel to London in 1917 to the High Court, to obtain a divorce, for which, the records show, she herself paid.

I wish that I had known her - she must have been a very spirited woman.

TIGERS IN LLANTEG

At one time, until about the end of the 1940s, travelling circuses were a regular seasonal sight on our roads. The more dangerous wild animals such as lions and tigers were carried securely in brightly-coloured cages covered with canvas flaps, while larger and more docile beasts like camels and elephants were led on foot, and were a great advertising attraction.

Hugh James, of Arfryn, recalls one of these circuses passing through Llanteg one summer some time in the 1920s, when he was about eight years old and his brother Verdi about ten. The convoy of cages and wagons, drawn by horses and traction engines, was travelling overnight from Carmarthen to Pembroke, or perhaps Tenby, and arrived in Llanteg at between four and five o'clock in the morning. Here the whole circus paused to give its two elephants a rest, and a request was made of Hugh's father, Howard James, to be allowed to water them in the large pond between Middleton and Blackheath (now filled in).

In return, Mr James asked the circus master if there were any of the animals his sons would be able to see; and accordingly the two little boys, Hugh and Verdi, were woken and brought down in the early dawn to be shown a large cage. Its canvas covering was rolled up for them to look inside, and there behind the bars lay two magnificent tigers.

"I never dreamed then," says Hugh, "that one day I would end up in the land of the tigers when I did my war service in Burma."

THE JAMES FAMILY OF BROOMYLAKE

by Hugh and Mollie James

William James and his wife Mary lived at Broomylake (or Brimylake) from around 1850 and their family of seven children were brought up there.

The family consisted of Thomas who lived and worked in Bristol - he also went to South Africa where he was involved in building a church; Sarah, who married and lived at the Parsonage, Amroth; Lewis, who lived and worked in Cardiff and was a Clerk of Works on the Civic Buildings; John, who died aged 21 years; Catherine, who lived in Bristol; Jenet, who died aged 21 years; and Alfred who married and continued in his father's trade of mason.

In 1896 Alfred built a new house to replace the old Broomylake. There he and his wife Elizabeth brought up their family of three boys and one girl - Howard, Evelyn, Herbert and William.

Broomylake remained in the family until the late nineteen-seventies.

Alfred James was the first pupil at Crunwere School, attending on his own for two weeks before the official opening. On leaving school he began working with his father, his first job being at Rose Cottage. The first contract he undertook on his own was the building at the bottom of the yard at Summerbrook. Evidence of his work is abundant in the area. He and his men built Blackheath, Middleton, Woodfield, Amroth Vicarage, Elidyr Cottage, Princes Gate Mission Room, Bryn-Sion School and many more.

THE DAVIES FAMILY OF BLACKHEATH

by Hugh and Mollie James

William Davies was born at Broomylake (or Brimylake) in 1840. His parents were James and Jane Davies. William married Mary Thomas of Prendergast, Haverfordwest, in Crunwere Church on August 30th 1866. At first they lived at Furzy Park, then at Broomylake, before moving to Blackheath. At the time this was a two-roomed cottage, but in 1913 the present Blackheath was built. The old cottage still stands alongside the house of today.

William and Mary Davies had a family of eight girls and three boys:- Anne (Mathias) Pendeilo, Amroth; Sarah (Beynon) The Gorse, Lampeter Velfrey; Catherine (Phillips) Middleton, Llanteg; James Davies, Lampeter Velfrey and Whitland; John Davies, Kidwelly; Jennet Elizabeth (Allen) Rose Cottage, Llanteg; Alice (Philipps) Upper Mead, Amroth; Martha (Mears) St Mary's Street, Whitland; Thomas Davies, who died young; Lucy

(Jones) Abergwili, Carmarthen; and Mary Emily (James) Blackheath, Llanteg.

Blackheath was home to William and Mary for as long as they lived, and after their days it was home to Howard and Emily James and their family until the nineteen-seventies.

HOME REMEDIES REMEMBERED

"The Lord hath created medicines out of the earth, and he that is wise will not abhor them" - herbalist Nicholas Culpeper quoting the Book of Ecclesiastes.

Mrs Betty Bevan - was given elderberry wine for colds.

Miss Ruth Bevan - was given Syrup of Figs. She had 'Vick' for her chest and olive oil "to put on your joints. And you weren't supposed to wash your hair before going out in the cold".

Mrs Margaret Carter - for a 'tickly' cough the juice of a lemon, mixed very thoroughly with honey and vinegar - this mixture would be kept warm on the side of the stove. For nettle stings, rub the area with a dock leaf.

Mr Ronnie Glanville - Syrup of Figs every week after a bath by the fire. Goose grease was used on a piece of flannel for colds on the chest.

Mr Glyn James - also remembers having goose grease on flannel and being given senna pods as a laxative which would make you do "100 yards in 10 seconds!" Another unique concoction - "take 1 pint of water and boil, skim and strain. Make pills out of the fat. Take two after you go to sleep and three before you wake up!"

Mr Desmond Wolff - "during a game of tag or similar with another young lad around the school area, we were negotiating a hedge when a blackthorn penetrated my leg. The whole thorn had gone in below the surface of the skin, and some half-hearted explorations with a pin was unsuccessful. My friend said that I should try the skin of an egg. Somewhat mystified, I asked if he meant the shell; he said no, I should break an egg and pull the skin (membrane) from the inside of the shell.

I went into the house and did that, placing a patch of the membrane, sticky side down, over the thorn area, where it quickly dried to form a shell-like cover. This was left on until the following day, the idea being that it would 'draw' the thorn out. Next day I removed the patch by wetting it with water and found the top of the thorn to be slightly above the surface, from where it was easily removed.

I don't know whether this always works but it certainly worked for me on that occasion."

Mr Wolff's mother was a firm believer in homeopathic medicine, so family ailments were treated with pills or tinctures having romantic-sounding names such as belladonna, arnica, aconite, nux vomica and so on.

'MISS GEORGIE' OF OAKLANDS: A VILLAGE CHARACTER

by Judith Lloyd

Georgiana Maria Philipps was born in India, probably Madras, in June 1859. She is known to have been living at Oaklands in 1881 (then aged 22) a daughter of the Philipps family who were noted here in the censuses of 1881 and 1891. Her father was Captain Lloyd Rice Philipps, late 33rd Madras Infantry, who gave his occupation in the 1881 census as farmer.

The family were related to the Morgans of Trenewydd and of Heatherland. An envelope containing photographs of Crunwere Church taken before its restoration in 1876 noted: "I am sending on the enclosed. I am sure you will like to have them and compare with (the) church these days. They were given to me by an old friend Mrs Jones, then of Lamphey Vicarage - (she) was I think a Miss Morgan of Trenewydd years ago and a cousin of Miss Phillip (*sic*) of Oakland. Mrs Jones took a great part in the restoration and gave well to the cause."

After the deaths of her parents in 1908 Georgiana - always known as Miss Georgie - appears to have taken in lodgers at Oaklands, and during the inter-war years she ran a shop there selling sweets and cigarettes. Among the domestic servants employed in the house was Joan Evans of Mountain Farm, who remembers coming to work in service at Oaklands in 1943 when she left school aged 14.

Towards the end of the Second World War, Geoffrey and Audrey James, newly wed, came to live at Oaklands and cared for Miss Georgie in return for their tenancy. The old lady was then living in the downstairs front room, an arrangement which lasted until her death in 1948.

Before the Jameses came, she had been in the care of a series of 'minders'. Audrey James says that Miss Georgie was very poor and the house shabbily furnished. When they first came she and Geoffrey had found the place overrun with vermin and Miss Georgie herself alive with fleas and in a state of physical neglect. She suffered badly with cataracts of the eyes, and Mr Wolff, the village schoolmaster, regularly used to come to read to her and do her correspondence.

The following notice appeared in the *Narberth Weekly News* on 27 June 1946:

87 years young.
Congratulations to Miss G.M.Philipps,
Oaklands, Amroth Road, Llanteg,
on reaching the ripe age of 87 years this week.
Although handicapped by failing eyesight,
Miss Philipps takes an active interest in parish affairs.

Miss Georgie died on 13th June 1948, in her 90th year. The funeral took place at Crunwere Church three days afterwards, and she was laid to rest in the churchyard.

Later that same year, Oaklands was bought by Geoffrey and Audrey James.

THE DAVIES FAMILY OF BEVLIN AND SPARROWS NEST

by John Davies

Elizabeth Davies was born at Bevlin and lived there all her life. She died in 1849 aged 100 years and was buried in Crunwere churchyard. In latter years she had been classed as a pauper.

Her son John David (note the change of surname) was born in 1793 at Bevlin and farmed Mountain Corner as well as renting various pieces of land around the village (the rents at this time were collected by the local vicar). John went on to marry a girl from St Issells, Sarah, who died in 1877 aged 92 years and is buried at Crunwere. John and Sarah had six children, one being Lewis David who was born in 1829.

Lewis married Theodosia, a daughter of Ben James, the blacksmith at Llanddowror. Theodosia bore Lewis ten children and died aged 55 years in 1877. Lewis married his second wife, Ann Parry (daughter of Thomas Parry, a mason living at the Coachlands) and had another two sons, James and William Davies (for some reason the surname changes back again). For many years Lewis worked at Pembroke Dock shipyards. Lewis and several others from the village would walk all the way to Pembroke Dock to start work at 7.30am, and walk back again each evening.

William married Sophia Maria Willday, daughter of Ralph Willday, a soldier living at the Folly, Llanteg. They resided at Abbey Stream, Ludchurch. William was killed in action in World War One and has a memorial plate in Ludchurch Church.

His brother James at 21 years was a servant at Cilrhiw, Princes Gate. He took Sparrows Nest on rent from the Colby Lodge Estate, agreeing to work there as it was a tied cottage. The cottage had 9 acres of mountain land at the time. James was a gardener at the Big House at Colby, and during the winter months he would do manual work around the estate farms. In 1901 James married Margretta James (daughter of John James the roadman who lived at Ruel Wall). Several of her brothers left the land and worked on the railways, except William James who later lived at Cartref, Tavernspite and was known as 'Will the Jockey'. Will had left to join the railway too, but changed his mind when he met a local farmer on Whitland river bridge who offered him the job of breaking a horse.

James and Margretta Davies
Photo: Alan Mason

James and Margretta lived their lives out at Sparrows Nest and had seven children, two dying young during the 1920s. 'Jim Sparrow', as he was affectionately known, was a devout churchgoer. He was Church Warden for many years and built most of the churchyard wall. He was a little short man, expert at using a scythe, and acted as 'second man' when working in the fields. (A less experienced farmworker would be 'first man' in the line and the 'second man' would keep him moving along.)

In those days six men would be used to work on a six-acre field and were expected to do an acre each per day. Jim was very good at keeping his scythe sharpened, and his expertise apparently generated a bit of jealousy from the 'first man', who bet Jim a week's wages (which was 10 shillings in about 1911, the time of this story) that come the day after tomorrow he himself would be 'second man' in place of Jim.

Now his underhand scheme was to slip a Cascara tablet *(strong laxative)* into Jim's tea. By 10am Jim was starting to suffer the effects, and by lunchtime he was even worse. However, with a family of young children to feed he couldn't afford to lose his wages, so he simply took off his trousers and carried on working regardless. At least he never lost the bet...

When Jim Sparrow died in 1953 his burial was delayed a few days so that the Archdeacon of St David's could officiate at the funeral. His wife Margretta died in 1964 aged 84 years. Their daughter Pattie, a spinster, taught at the Sunday School for many years.

Worker Unrest at Llanteg.

The first mechanical horse-drawn mower came to Trenewydd Farm between 1915 and 1918. With no work to do, the men from the village stayed at home, forced to listen to the machine rattling along (the most noise they had ever heard) and losing them their wages of a shilling (five pence) a day. They decided to sabotage the 'monster' by placing iron pegs in the crop of hay. The next day silence reigned again. The local blacksmith had been warned not to repair the mower, and so on the third day the farmer had to come and ask the men to return to work and do the mowing with their scythes. This was a great relief to them and the mowing machine remained out of action for that season.

Llanteg during the Second World War.

Three Scottish Divisions were stationed in the Ruel Wall, Craig-y-Borion and Colby Lodge areas during the War. The men disembarked from trains at St Clears and marched five abreast down through Llanteg. There were searchlights at the top of Craig-y-Borion and Rosemary Lane.

At that time you were not supposed to put up a tent, but being young boys a few decided to erect one in the woods which at that time grew near Sparrows Nest (where Hazeldene now stands). They were in for a shock when confronted with soldiers with weapons who assumed they were the enemy!

First Motor Car

Motor traffic was once so seldom seen in the countryside that around 1916 an entire family came out to await the arrival of the first motor car through Llanteg after seeing a man walking ahead along the road with flags. *(A law of 1831 required a man to precede a 'horseless carriage' with a red flag. The law was repealed in 1895, but as this reminiscence shows, the practice continued as a safety precaution - editor.)*

MEMORIES OF MY GREAT-AUNT MILDRED GARRETT (nee PHILLIPS)

by Ruth Roberts

Mildred was born in December 1900 at Middleton, which was then just a small cottage in what is now the garden. She attended Crunwere School with her two sisters and two brothers. According to the Admittance Register she left at fourteen when she reached the age limit and began domestic service. The house which was to become the present-day Middleton was built around the beginning of the First World War. Mildred, along with her sister Gladys, went to work at Amroth Castle, and she also worked at Sodson House, Narberth. Millie, as she was known, trained as a psychiatric nurse in Barnwood House, Gloucester, and would often talk of the "dear people" she met there and who affectionately called her "Nurse Phillipie". She was forced to return home after contracting T.B., the disease which killed her fiancé. Millie had the ability to see phantom funerals and other such things; and her brother Tom recalled that as a youth whilst cycling down the Stoney Road towards the Captain's Pond a black ghost dog ran across his path and through the spokes of his bike without him feeling any impact.

Middleton Farming Group - early 1930s **Photo: Ruth Roberts**

1960s.

Throughout her life Millie had been a devoted member of Crunwere Church, where generations of the family are buried. Saturday afternoon would usually be taken up with picking flowers from the garden to be placed on the family's numerous graves. Millie played the organ at Crunwere Church for many years, although she had only been able to afford a few lessons in her youth and was mainly self-taught. During her later years she ran the farm with her brother Lel (*Leslie*) and sister Peggy (*Florence*). Until the late 1960s they were still milking by hand. They also made their own bread, which they had done since running a small shop in their parlour in the 1930s. The flour was bought in large sacks which, when empty, would be made into pillow cases and tea towels (there was also still a 'rag rug' in the bedroom).

Millie had a garden in part of a field behind the house which bordered onto the 'Roman Road'. Here she would grow potatoes and peas. She also had a well-stocked garden at the side of the house where she did some topiary figures on top of the hedges.

To supplement their income they took in bed-and-breakfast guests during the summer as at that time holiday-makers would often be unable to find vacancies in Tenby and would have to search all the way back to Llanteg. Many people returned year after year. There was no bathroom, only a flush toilet outside the back door, and so hot water for washing had to be carried up to the rooms in jugs every morning. Millie would often vacate her room if they were very busy and sleep in a little room just off the back kitchen - 'the glory hole'.

Millie was an active member of the Women's Institute and enjoyed singing and acting. After her brother Leslie died in the 1970s Millie had a pet pig, Harvey, which was very tame but which eventually grew too large for the house. She remained single until her 77th year when she married Jack Garrett at Mountain Chapel. (*It is reputed that Millie saw a fortune teller when she was young who told her that she would marry in her later years, and this was something that she had always firmly believed.*)

LLANTEG YOUNG FARMERS' CLUB

Llanteg Young Farmers ran for many years and held a varied programme of events as can be seen from the following extracts from the minutes for 1949/50:

The Annual meeting was held at the Church Hall (*old school*) on 4th October 1949 when Mr Hawes was elected as president with Mr George Lawrence as chairman. It was decided that in future meetings would be held fortnightly. On January 3rd 1950 a Social was held at the Church Hall: music was provided by Miss Jean Richards who had kindly lent her gramophone, and by Walter Morgans who accompanied with his piano accordian. On the 21st February a debate was held on '*Should blood sports be abolished*?' After a lively discussion it was decided that they should not.

The Y.F.C. Rally was to be held in Tenby on May 15th and it was decided that Llanteg would enter the following competitions:- Scarecrow Making, Horse Handling, Tractor Reversing, Demonstration of Craft Work, Splicing, Shearing, Identification of Weeds and Grasses, Dairying and Cookery.

LLANTEG HOME GUARD

The Local Defence Volunteers were founded in May 1940, but because the initials L.D.V. were jokingly taken to mean '**L**ook, **D**uck and **V**anish' the name was changed to the 'Home Guard'. They were formed as a precaution against invasion and the group, comprising Amroth, Llanteg and Tavernspite, was known as 'F Company'. They were based at Llanteglos, in one of the henhouses. *(Llanteglos was owned by Grismond Williams. Before the War he had five or six sheds of poultry and employed eight to ten local people including Millie Phillips Middleton, Pattie Davies Sparrows Nest, Arthur George The Downs and Tommy Glanville.)*

The Captain of the Company was Mr Jack Mortimer, Summerbrook (ex First World War) assisted by Lt. Pryce Evans, Llanteglos (a former London Police Inspector). The Sergeants were Leslie Glanville, William Henry James and Frankie James (all ex First World War). Dr D.H.Pennant, the local G.P. and ex First World War, was also closely involved. They were a succesful group and Jack Mortimer was an excellent leader.

The Amroth Watch was based at Crayes Billiard Room over the shop (*now Toad Hall*) and Lt. Lawrence Hughes, Blackhall, was in charge. Some six or eight of the men would be on beach patrol from dusk until dawn, duties also including two-man patrols from New Inn to Penglyn. The men always carried their Winchester rifles with the ammunition in their holster - never 'one up the spout' as it was called (*loaded*). Only on one occasion were they ordered to do patrol with loaded rifles: evidently 'something' was expected to be coming in from Ireland, and although nothing occurred that night at Amroth it was later heard on the grapevine that they had 'got their man'. The men had to make their own way down to Amroth for the watch but would be brought back home at 6.30 to 7am in Hitchings's lorry or van.

Mr Wyn Lawrence of Trelissy was surprised to be one of only ten men from Pembrokeshire selected to attend the Stand Down Parade in Hyde Park at 3pm on 3rd December 1944. The Parade consisted of 7000 men who marched about seven miles. It was a very cold day but Mr Lawrence says they found it very warm with their great coats buttoned up. After the march the men were entertained to a concert at the Albert Hall. Mr Lawrence saw the King there but remembers that he "was not much to look at.... a bit of a disappointment".

Mr Lawrence went on to receive a Certificate of Appreciation of Good Service and a special commendation for his loyal and excellent service.

SOME LLANTEG SERVICEMEN AND WOMEN REMEMBERED

Norman Allen, Oxford - Served with the R.A.F. in a Bomb Disposal Unit in the Second World War.

W. T. Allen, Private, W.W.I., Rose Cottage
Photo: Hugh James

W.T.Allen, Rose Cottage - Served as a Medical Orderly in a military hospital in London during the First World War.

A. H. Brinsden, Corporal, W.W.2., Stanwell
Photo: Tony Brinsden

Albert Henry Brinsden, Stanwell - Bert Brinsden was called up in September 1939, and throughout the Second World War served in the Royal Air Force. He was demobilised in 1946. During his service he was stationed at various R.A.F Stations in this country, mainly in and around London, but also at Invergorden in northern Scotland. Bert was a driver of all types of R.A.F vehicles, including the 60 foot long *Queen Mary* aircraft transporter vehicles. During his service he was promoted to Corporal.

A. George, L.A.C., W.W.2., The Downs
Photo: Ken George

Arthur George, The Downs - Was an R.A.F. reservist and was called up early in 1940. He first served as a Ground Gunner and in 1942 when the R.A.F. Regiment was formed he was a member of its first squadron. However following an accident at Linton-on-Ouse in Yorkshire Mr George was regraded to Storeman and spent the rest of the War at R.A.F. Pembrey and Pembroke Dock before being demobbed in 1945 at the age of 42 (old compared to the age of the average serviceman). His daughter Mary recalls visiting him by train when he underwent an operation in a Gloucester hospital.

R. G. George, Private, W.W.I., The Downs
Photo: Ken George

R.G.George, The Downs - Gwilym was a Private in the First World War. He served in France and was very badly gassed on the Somme, suffering the ill effects for the rest of his life. He died aged 52 after a short illness whilst working as Chief Cashier for Wimpy Ltd at Port Talbot. He was a very good writer and could write the Lord's Prayer in a circle the size of a silver three-penny bit.

Hugh Slader Glanville, Lanteg - Served as a Private with the 24th Welsh Regiment. He died at Gaza of wounds received in battle, 11th November 1917, aged 25 years, and is buried at Beersheba.

Miss Margaret Hawes, Heatherland (later Mrs Carter) - An A.T.S. subaltern, she served in the F.A.N.Y.s. Towards the end of the Second World War was in the B.E.F., where she was in command of ambulances, working day and night carrying casualties from ambulance trains etc. to airfields and ports, and latterly overseeing the transport of German casualties to trains returning them to Germany.

C. James, Gunner, W.W.I., Summerbrook
Photo: Graham Mortimer

Frank James, The Cabin - Frank served at Ypres with the South Wales Borderers in the First World War.

F. James, Private, W.W.I.
The Cabin
Photo: Glyn James

W. G. James, Gunner, W.W.2.,
Bevlin
Photo: Audrey James

Geoffrey James, Bevlin - Audrey James writes: "My late husband Geoffrey enlisted in the Royal Artillery in March 1940 at the age of 19 years. After carrying out basic training, his first posting was the coastal town of Towyn, on the north Welsh coast. Later on he had a number of postings along the south coast of England, where he was a gunner operating anti-aircraft guns ('Bofors') which were used to defend the wartime aerodromes and industrial targets.

Whilst carrying out these duties he was injured by shrapnel from an explosion within the gun magazine. Whilst recovering from his injuries he worked as a plotter, which involved the co-ordination of activities between the Royal Air Force, Royal Artillery and the Luftwaffe.

In 1943 Geoff's unit was posted to the Manchester area to defend the factories that were engaged in the manufacture of munitions and tanks. It was here that he contracted diphtheria and spent some weeks at Davyhume Isolation Hospital. Whilst he was here in hospital his Battalion was mobilised to south-east Asia and Singapore. Some weeks later he was to discover that the majority of his unit had been captured by the Japanese. Most of these men he did not see again.

However, in the early seventies whilst we were shopping in Haverfordwest, a man called out Geoff's Royal Artillery identification number from across the street. Despite the passing years they both recognised each other, and Geoff responded by calling out his friend's identification number. Their meeting had a deeper significance, since they had both enlisted together at Llanelli and became instant friends. This friend's name was Gwyn Rex. He had been a prisoner of war with the Japanese for a number of years, and when liberated by the Americans he weighed only 4½ stone. A lot of their wartime pals had not survived."

H. G. James, Gunner, W.W.2., Bevlin
Photo: Glyn James

Glyn James, Bevlin - Glyn was a driver in World War Two, and did his training at Harwick and Chesterfield. He recalls: "we did eight weeks non-stop training. We had to do a two-mile assault course before breakfast, one mile out and one back. We were five to a tent and slept 'feet to pole'. We trained for river crossings and did route marches, starting off at five miles and building up to thirty miles with a 95lb pack on our back". Later at Ringway Aerodrome, Manchester, Glyn earned 2/6 extra a week by volunteering to be a 'Judas' - which meant being the first to make a jump with a parachute to encourage the other trainees to follow. Glyn reckons he did this over a hundred times in all.

H. R. James, L.A.C., W.W.2., Blackheath
Photo: Betty James

Herbert James, Blackheath - Joined the R.A.F. in July 1942. After his training he went on a Fitter 2A course for some weeks. On completion he had embarkation leave and then was posted to north Africa, serving at Casablanca, Algiers, and various other bases. At the end of the war he was posted to Italy, and finally came back to St. Athan's for a few months before being demobbed.

H. James, Gunner, W.W.I., Blackheath (Inset—wife, Emily)
Photo: Hugh James

Howard James, Blackheath - In 1915 and 1916 Howard worked in Blaengwynfi as a shorer strengthening the tunnel walls in the mines. In early 1917 he joined the Royal Artillery and was sent to Athlone in Ireland for a few months before being ordered to France. There he moved around the battle fronts in France and Belgium. He was released from duty in March 1919.

W. H. James, Gunner, W.W.2, Blackheath
Photo: Hugh James

Hugh James, Blackheath - Joined the Royal Artillery in January 1940 and over the next months received training as a Gunner/Driver at several army bases in England. He was in Woolwich in August 1942 when the Regiment was posted overseas. Troops were moved by train to Greenwich and embarked on the *Rangitata*, leaving the Clyde on August 28th 1942 in a large convoy for an unknown destination. Their first port of call was Freetown, Sierra Leone. Their next was Durban where they had a short break before re-embarking and sailing on to India. On arrival in Bombay they were sent by train across country to north-east India, reaching Assam on the Burma border by November 1942. There the troops became part of the 23rd Indian Division and prepared for the expected Japanese offensive along the Chindwin. There was intense fighting over the mountain ranges around Imphal and Kohima, with some of the hill tops changing hands several times. For three and a half months they were cut off from contact with the outside world except by air, in the siege of Imphal. The Japanese were defeated at Kohima at the end of May 1944; the road to Imphal was reopened and the enemy driven back over the Chindwin and out of Burma. Hugh arrived back in Southampton on the last day of 1945, returning to Llanteg on January 1st 1946.

W. James, Gunner, W.W.I., Broomylake
Photo: Hugh James

William James, Broomylake - Joined the Royal Artillery on 31st May 1916. In the October after training he was sent to France and by December was in the Heavy Artillery Group based in St. Quentin. He remained there until the end of the war and came home on January 25th 1919.
G.S.G.Jones, Heatherland - Major Jones was with the Canadian Tanks during the Second World War and took part in the raid on Dieppe.
N.J.G.Jones, Heatherland - Colonel Jones served in the Indian Army during the Second World War and was with the 4th Indian Division in the Middle East.

J. E. J. Mason, A.B.R.N., W.W.2, Ruelwall
Photo: Alan Mason

James Edgar John Mason, Ruelwall - Mr Mason was a Stoker 1st Class in the Royal Navy. Whilst ferrying the troops in for the Normandy landings on 12th June 1944, he was killed in action at the age of 23, dying just two weeks before his son Alan's first birthday. He has no grave, but his name is recorded on a memorial at Chatham in Kent.

D. Mortimer, W.A.A.F., W.W.2, Summerbrook
Photo: Graham Mortimer

Donna Mortimer, Summerbrook - Served in the W.A.A.F. in the Second World War as a wireless operator, both in Lincolnshire and at Blackpool.

J. S. Mortimer, Sergeant, W.W.I., Ledgerland
Photo: Graham Mortimer

J.S.Mortimer, Ledgerland - Served with the Pembrokeshire Yeomanry as a Sergeant in the First World War. They took their own horses, riding them from Penally to Carmarthen Station. On passing through Llanteg someone came out from the Folly and gave Mr Mortimer a couple of pennies - "everyone was very patriotic then", comments his son Graham. Mr Mortimer went to Norfolk before travelling to Palestine. Among others from this area were Private H.Jones, Heatherland, and Private H.S.Glanville, Llanteg. The Pembrokeshire Yeomanry helped to liberate Jerusalem and later, in December 1917, Jericho. It was hailed as "one of the most brilliant feats of arms of the British Army in the Great War". The weather conditions were appalling and at times the animals and wheeled transport could not move for the mud. Even the camel ration trains could not get through, with many of the camels dying of the wet and cold. The regiment was recalled to the Western Front in France in May 1918. After returning on the *Arcadian* Mr Mortimer was so seriously injured on 21st September 1918 that his father was called to his bedside. He spent many months in hospital both in London and at Rockwood Hospital, Cardiff.

John Garfield Phelps, Milton Back - Served with the R.A.F. during the Second World War and was medically discharged.

David Phillips - 'Dai The Corner' - Served in the First World War as a Gunner, Pembroke Royal Garrison Artillery. While serving in France in April 1917 he received severe gunshot wounds, and despite a number of operations his left leg had to be amputated. He returned home to Llanteg on 15th February 1918.

T. W. Phillips, Sapper, W.W.I.,
The Corner
Photo: Hugh James

D. Wolff, W.O., R.A.F., W.W.2,
School House
Photo: Desmond Wolff

Desmond Wolff, School House - "In late 1940 I applied for aircrew training in the R.A.F. and was told to report to Cardington in Bedfordshire to appear before a selection board. Things went well enough except that, in completing the form of application, I had included details of my mother's illness when answering the question on health of parents. There followed some prodding by the medics, and I was later informed that I had not been accepted due to a medical query. (Some months later, when firmly in the R.A.F., I received a letter saying that the situation had been re-assesed and would I apply again.)

In March 1941 I approached the problem from another angle, going to London and R.A.F. Uxbridge. Wiser now, I omitted a few details concerning family health and was accepted for training as a pilot.

Induction was at Aircrew Receiving Centre, St. John's Wood, London. We marched to meals at Regents Park Zoo, where visitors seemed to be more interested in us than in the animals at feeding time. This was not too surprising, since for several days we had part civilian clothing and part uniform, Stores dept. being hard pressed at the time. And so to inoculations, P.T., 'square bashing', lectures and general familiarisation with the Service.

From ACRC we were posted to Initial Training Wing at Paignton in Devon. More P.T. and square bashing, alternating with ground subjects. No sign of an aircraft, but at the end of the course we were issued with flying kit. Classes were held in Oldway Mansion, which had been the home of the Singer family of sewing-machine fame.

From ITW we went to Wilmslow, near Manchester, where we learnt that our next destination would be Canada. We boarded ship at Greenock in Scotland and arrived several days later at Halifax, Nova Scotia. There followed many days on the train to a base near Calgary, Alberta: this was to Elementary Flying Training School, where we came to grips with Tiger Moth training aircraft. Flying alternated with classes and we were kept too busy to get out much, but I remember thinking on my first visit to Calgary that several new colours had been invented. After the blackout at home, it was a remarkable experience to see all the city lights and flashing neon signs. The people of Canada were always wonderfully friendly and welcoming.

When we had been suitably beaten into shape the course split up, some going to Service Flying Training School on single-engined Harvard aircraft, and some going - as I did - to SFTS on twin-engined Oxford aircraft. These two locations had the admirable names of Moose Jaw and Medicine Hat respectively.

At the completion of SFTS successful pupils were awarded their 'wings'.

From SFTS we went to Prince Edward Island to practice navigation over the sea. Our next stop was Operational Training Unit at Greenwood, Nova Scotia, where we converted onto Lockheed Hudson aircraft and teamed up with others to form crews. Our navigator was from London and two Canadian lads were in the category of wireless operator/air gunner: they would alternate duties during flights. As always, there were more classes and exams.

On completion of OTU we were on the move again, by ship to England and a posting to Lyneham in Wiltshire. There we were allocated a Hudson, which we ferried to Rabat in Morocco. The aircraft went to a maintenance unit and we went to a holding unit near Algiers. From there we joined a Coastal Command operational squadron near Oran, flying on anti-submarine patrols and convoy escort.

In due course we transferred to Gibraltar, where we converted onto a heavier type of aircraft, the Ventura, which was like a big brother of the Hudson. This type had an efficient radar, so it was important for the wireless operator, who also monitored the radar, to be able to change over with the gunner, as peering into a screened radar scope was hard on the eyes.

Operations to the west were over the Atlantic, those to the east were over the Mediterranean. By this stage we had acquired a co-pilot.

From Gibraltar we moved eastwards again to bases along the North African coast, until we moved to Italy, where the squadron changed to a different type of aircraft and a different type of operation. As we were at about the end of our tour we were posted to a communications flight in the Naples area. From this base we flew VIPs to various destinations in various countries.

On one such flight we were staying overnight in Corsica. It was May 7th 1945 and unofficial news came through of victory in Europe. Next day we flew back to Naples and learnt that VE-day was official. We continued with the Comm. flight until the slow process of demobilisation began. On return to England I opted to stay on in the Service for a while and was posted to Leuchars in Scotland, flying as staff pilot for pupil navigators.

From there my last station was Tern Hill in Shropshire, and finally to a demobilisation centre, by which time the year was 1947."

Kathleen Wolff, School House - She went first to Wilmslow on joining the W.A.A.F. during World War Two, then was posted to Pembroke Dock, being accommodated for a short while in Defensible Barracks. From there she moved to Angle, then back to Pembroke Dock and finally to Plymouth, living at Mount Batten and working at Mount Wise.

Sheila Wolff, School House - In World War Two Sheila served at Leighton Buzzard in Bedfordshire, Russell Square in London and St. Athan, Cardiff, where she was assistant adjutant and gas officer (not as sinister as it sounds). In her final year in the W.A.A.F. she was married and was thenceforth known as Flight Officer Martin.

For a complete list of serving personnel in both World Wars see Appendix.

A WAR BABY'S MEMORIES OF LLANTEG IN THE 'FORTIES

by Tony Brinsden

What did you do during the War? was a question I often heard during my childhood. As one who was conceived just prior to the commencement of hostilities in the Second World War my memories of it are not too clear, and my answer to the question would be "Eat and sleep mainly". However what memories I have I shall try to recount here, and also my memories of immediate Post War life and activities in Llanteg.

At that time Llanteg was a much smaller village than it is now with all the houses well spaced out, the majority of them being engaged in agriculture to some degree. I was born and raised in Stanwell which was then being farmed by my grandparents. My mother had returned home there at the start of the war (having previously been in service in Berkshire which is where she had met my father), my father being then away serving in the Royal Air Force. Stanwell was a two-bedroomed house so I shared a room in my early years with my mother.

Greenacre, which is now a ruin, had been my grandparents' home prior to their moving to Stanwell just before the war. It was then in reasonable condition and was still part furnished, but was unfortunately severely damaged by fire when it was used as a shelter by army personnel who were training in the area at that time. I well remember one soldier regularly used to call at Stanwell for a cup of tea and to warm himself whilst on guard duty. I also remember hearing the convoys of lorries travelling along the main road to the various Pembrokeshire Barracks and on a couple of occasions being hustled into the house very quickly because there were enemy aircraft passing overhead.

One incident, nothing to do with Llanteg, but nevertheless which sticks in my mind, was when I travelled to High Wycombe, Bucks, with my mother to stay for a few days close to where my father was stationed. She and I were walking on High Wycombe Common when we were chased by army tanks who were exercising on the Common. It was probably a light relief for the tank crews but it was a frightening experience for a 3 or 4 year old. I also recall on the return train journey that the train was held up outside Swansea because of a heavy bombing raid over the city.

During the war years birthday parties were unheard of, as were any kind of party, and Christmas was a very austere affair. There were no lavish presents as there are today and all food was rationed. This did not stop us having a fine feast for Christmas lunch which would have been a cockerel killed for the occasion served with all home garden grown vegetables. My Christmas presents usually consisted of a book, pencil, game, apple, orange and a small Dinky toy - these things meant the world to a child in those days. The Christmas of 1944 or 1945 is especially remembered for a toy that I received as a present. It was a model of an American Willys Jeep measuring about 9 inches long and propelled by an old gramophone motor. It was steerable by a small steering wheel and even had lights. This wonderful present had been hand-made for me by my uncle, Bob Davies, who was working at the Gloster Aero Company, Gloucester, developing the first jet propelled aircraft. This jeep was my pride and joy for many years - if only I had kept it!

As with all Service personnel during the war my father had very little home leave and consequently I was almost six before I got to know him. My uncle Bob used to come home a little more often from Gloucester and it was always a great occasion when either came home. Petrol was rationed and virtually unobtainable and so Bob used to cycle home on some occasions for just a day or so. On other occasions he might be lucky and get enough petrol to mix with paraffin to enable him to come home on his motor cycle. My father would usually come home by train to either Whitland or Kilgetty station.

Reggie's Garage **Photo: Doreen Glanville**

There was no television in those days, not in Llanteg anyway, and news broadcasts by John Snagg were listened to on a daily basis on the old wireless. These were quite large affairs and were connected to a long aerial which ran from the house to a copper beech tree on the lawn. They were run off two batteries, one a dry battery and the other a wet rechargeable accumulator. The accumulators were recharged on an engine and generator by Reggie Glanville at his garage at Llanteg Cross as there was no mains electricity in the village during the war - indeed it didn't arrive until the early 1950s. I don't know what the life of one of these accumulators was, but I think that they had to be charged up at least weekly and perhaps more often.

Long winter evenings were spent in front of an open fire reading or playing board or card games. The only source of light was either from an oil (paraffin) lamp or candles. The oil lamps were usually used downstairs whilst a much smaller one or a candle was used for the bedroom. Perhaps this was a good thing as every window had to have a blackout blind over it so that no chink of light was visible from outside. Every evening before retiring to bed the open fire would be stummed down with 'bawls' so that it would stay in overnight. The 'bawls' were a mixture of clay and coal dust which burned very slowly and also created a fair amount of dust. I remember that in the winter we lived in the front of the house but in the summer we lived in the back. Both the kitchen and the front room had open grates with an oven on one side and a water boiler on the other side. Almost all the cooking, including the baking of all the bread, was done on these fires and in the ovens although we also had a paraffin stove and oven to supplement them if necessary. The flour for making the bread was bought in 1cwt bags and when these were empty they would be used by my mother and grandmother as aprons.

Shopping in the wartime years was done locally, with 'Maggie the shop', at The Laurels where Mrs Maggie Bowen had the Post Office and General Grocery shop, or at the Co-op in Kilgetty which in those days was a mini department store selling everything from groceries to clothes, ironmongery and farm supplies. The journey to Kilgetty would be made by my mother on her pedal cycle or on Ebsworths buses which passed through the village on the main road three times a day. These buses would also be used by the Miss Phillipses of Middleton, the Miss Hodges of The Barriets (now Caldey View) and Miss Davies of Sparrowsnest to take their home grown produce and to sell it on the market in Tenby. All food at this time was severely rationed but we were lucky that we could overcome some of the hardships of food rationing by churning our own butter and killing a pig. This was strictly illegal but was practised on all of the farms. The bacon would be cured in salt in a large slate tub which was in the pantry, and then hung on hooks in the living room until it was used. The killing of a pig was a major event with many gallons of water having to be boiled to 'shave' the pig, then it would have to be hung for a few days before it was cut up and salted. The killing of pigs would be staggered around the neighbours so that only one at a time would be killed in the locality. After the making of faggots etc. these together with the fry would be distributed to neighbours as there were no fridges or deep freezers in which to keep them.

In 1945 I started my schooldays in Crunwere School, now closed and a private dwelling house known as Sea Breeze. It was one classroom which was divided into two by portable screens. There were two teachers, Miss Herbert who taught the under 10s, and the headmaster Mr.Wolff who taught the older pupils. There was a big open fire on one wall of the room and this was the only form of heating that there was. I cannot recall how many pupils we were but I wouldn't think we were more than a dozen. We all had to walk to school regardless of the weather. Playtimes would be spent playing on the front yard with a ball or during the better weather in a small field behind the school. The games would be football, hide and seek, touch and marbles. At that time gypsies used to park their caravans in Allen's Lane at the side of the school whilst they travelled around the village selling their pegs and pots and pans. Whilst they were on their rounds they would leave some of their horses tethered in Allen's Lane and if there was no one around at lunch time or when school finished, some of the bigger boys would untether the horses and drive them down Allen's Lane into the Grassy Lane or down to the stream below Rose Cottage. We were naughty in those days but we didn't commit damage as is often the case today. In any case, anyone caught interfering with the gypsies' horses was immediately caned in front of all the pupils by Mr Wolff.

Another milestone in my life was reached at the end of 1945 when my father was demobilised from the Royal Air Force. He returned to live at Stanwell and had a job at the Proof and Experimental Station at Pendine. I remember it seeming funny at the time to have two men more or less permanently at home.

Further indelible memories were to come in 1946. In September of that year my grandfather died, and as a result my father gave up his job at Pendine to take over the running of Stanwell. Although it would not be a viable proposition today, in those days a living could be made and a family supported on 40 acres of land. Also at the end of 1946 Crunwere School closed and all of the pupils were transferred to Amroth School. I was quite lucky when this happened because Stanwell was situated more or less equidistant between the two schools but I now qualified for transport to and from school so no more wettings on bad days. The transport was provided in an ex-Army personnel carrier owned and driven by Mrs Annie Lewis of Penglyn, Amroth.

Amroth School was bigger than Crunwere had been and there were two playgrounds, one for the girls and one for the boys. There were also two fireplaces, albeit one was the old barrack room type stove. In those days the younger children were not given pen and paper until they were about seven years of age so we did all our schoolwork on slates using a thin slate stick as a pencil. The letters or figures so written could then easily be cleaned off the slate with a damp rag. None of the children in those days had fountain pens, and ball point pens were unheard of. The only pen used was a nibbed pen that was continually dipped into the inkwell on the desk. Games played during playtime at Amroth School were similar to those played at Crunwere.

In 1947, I think it was March or April, there was a terrific snowstorm. I recall I was ill and confined to my bed at the time but on the morning after the snow had fallen I was taken downstairs to be shown a 'snowman' inside the back kitchen door. This had been formed, almost in the perfect shape of a snowman by the blizzard driving the snow through the keyhole of the back door. The snow was so deep outside that you could be walking over the telegraph wires without knowing it.

In the 1940s there were not many tractors and even fewer cars in Llanteg. We had neither at Stanwell but there was an old Singer car which had part of its bodywork removed and a cart body bolted in its place which was used to drive out into the fields the farmyard manure and to gather in the hay at haymaking time. Haymaking time was quite an experience because when the hay was ready to be got in all the neighbours would turn up to help. It would not be unusual to have at least a dozen men sitting down around the hayrick for supper, and it was very interesting for a young boy to listen to the tales that were told although everything that was said was not fully understood! There were no balers at this time and all of the hay was manhandled on pitchforks. It was brought in from the field either on a horse and cart or a neighbour's tractor and trailer.

At Stanwell, as on most of the smallholdings in the area, the cows were milked by hand. The milk was poured into milk churns and these were collected on a daily basis by lorry from the United Dairies at Whitland. The milk lorries at first didn't go further than Stanwell, so every morning there would be a gathering of all the nearby farmers bringing their churns of milk to meet the milk lorry. They would also bring rabbits that had been caught by them to await collection by Bryn Davies of Whitland who used to buy them and then send them off to London and other big cities where there was a ready market for rabbit as meat was still rationed.

Towards the end of 1947 my uncle Bob returned to Llanteg from Gloucester and again gave me a present which was to give me many years of pleasure. It was a scooter that he had made as it was almost impossible to get a child's bicycle. A couple of years later I learned to ride my mother's bike and then Bob gave me one of his old racing bikes (which he still has). All of the children in the locality at that time used to cycle a great deal. The roads were virtually traffic free and there was very little danger for the younger cyclist. To give an example of the volume of traffic, one of the hobbies of the day was collecting car registration numbers. I would sit at the Folly Cross for possibly two or three hours and at the end of this would have perhaps ten to fifteen registration numbers to show for my troubles. If only that were the case today!

Towards the end of the 'forties some modernisation work was started at Stanwell. A new 12 bay cowshed was built with dairy and cattle food store attached (now converted to two holiday cottages). A milking machine was installed. This was powered by diesel engine as there was still no mains electricity in the village. In 1949 our first tractor, an Allis Chalmers, was purchased. This allowed my father and mother to extend their farming activities to include ploughing some of the land and growing some cereal and other crops which they had been unable to do before. Many of our neighbours also bought tractors for the first time around this period and were able to go along with the Ministry of Agriculture slogan of 'Plough more, Feed more'.

Although my parents were not overly religious Sundays were a day of rest. Only the necessary farm work would be carried out and church was attended at least once and sometimes twice. When I got a little older I also attended Sunday School. There were no school or Sunday School outings but there were special events during the year. There would be St. Margaret's Fair in Tenby in July. The whole of the Parade would be taken up by the fair and no traffic was allowed. Later in the year there were fairs at Whitland, St. Clears and Narberth. I would be taken to one of these at least once a year. If it was Whitland or Narberth I would have to ride on the carrier of mother's bike as there was no bus service to these towns. Another occasion in the year would be Amroth Big Day. If the weather was good, people would travel from miles around by horse and cart, car, tractor or bicycle to attend the sports and other activities or to bathe in the sea on this day.

During the 'forties holidays were virtually unheard of in Llanteg, none of the locals would even dream of taking a holiday. A few days at the beach might be snatched here and there throughout the summer, but never more than two or three. During school holidays I would stay for a few days with my aunt, uncle and cousin at Bethesda, just north of Narberth, or my cousin would stay with us at Stanwell and that is all the holidays I had until much later in my life. It was towards the end of the 'forties that holiday makers started returning to this area and then in very small numbers. There were no caravan sites anywhere in the area, these started to develop in the mid-fifties.

Although there had been a war up to 1945 and rationing had been maintained on most foodstuffs and clothes into the early 'fifties, and other consumables, including vehicles of all descriptions, were hard to come by, life for a child in this village was marvellous. I didn't have a television set to watch or a roomful of toys or a computer with fancy games to play with, but I was a very happy child. I don't recall being bored as you hear being glibly trotted out today as an excuse for the taking of drugs and other juvenile misdemeanours. Yes, we were naughty on occasions, we let off the odd firework where we shouldn't have or knocked on a door and ran, but we never caused any damage or anyone any harm. The village was a real country village with virtually every household engaged to a greater or lesser extent in agriculture, even if it only meant keeping a pig and a few hens. It was a quieter place with no need to lock doors and everyone understanding the needs and looking out for everyone else. Yes, times were hard as far as money and material things were concerned, but, despite everything, the 'forties were halcyon days for a child.

CRUNWERE NEWS

Death of an Octogenarian - on Friday January 30th 1914 an old and respected inhabitant passed away. Mr William Allen, Milton, was 87 years old and a native of the parish. He was born a short distance from the house where he died and spent the whole of his life in Crunwere.

Of a robust constitution and an active temperament, he was closely identified with the business life of the village in his earlier years, where he carried on a large smithy and also a grocery business. He was a well known character for many miles around.

The funeral took place on 3rd February at Crunwere Church. It was largely attended with many coming great distances. The duties of undertaker were efficiently carried out by Messrs Hodge Brothers, The Barriets.

Narberth, Whitland and Clynderwen News 12 Feb 1914

Welcome Home - on December 18th a meeting was held at the Schoolroom to welcome home 'another of the soldier lads' - Private William Howells, Woodreef. Notwithstanding the rough weather, the attendance was excellent. The Chairman, however, expressed his regret that Mr Howells "was the only one who had failed to attend the meeting".

Narberth Weekly News 1 Jan 1920

Personal - it is pleasing to learn that Mr Wilfred Davies, Milton, has been successful in securing a position in the Police Force and commences duties today (Thursday) at St. Helens, Lancashire.

Narberth Weekly News 22 Jan 1925

County Elections - the County Council electorate of Amroth division have three candidates for one seat; all are farmers and politically favour Conservatism:- Mr J.C.S. Glanville (present member), Mr Brown (Cold Blow) and Mr Davies, Trenewydd. Crunwere has the distinction of providing two of the candidates.

Narberth Weekly News 22 Jan 1925

Mothers' Union Concert - Friday last there was an excellent concert in the school by Crunwere Mothers' Union. The Secretary, Mrs Wolff, must be complimented on the organisation of the event, which with the necessary rehearsals entailed a large amount of work for all.

The 'Mothers' all performed admirably and the school was packed with an appreciative audience. A monologue was performed by Mrs Davies, Greenacre, and various other items took place. A few of those taking part were:- F.Wolff, Mrs York Glanville, Mr W.Allen, Mrs Howard James, Mr

L.Phillips, Mr J.Lewis and Miss S.Wolff.

At the close the chairman spoke in glowing terms of the all round excellency of the items.

Accompanying the performers were:- Miss Williams, Llanteglos, Mr Wolff, School House and Mr Howard James, Blackheath.

Narberth Weekly News 3 March 1927

Crunwere Band of Hope - on Wednesday of last week a meeting was held at Mountain Chapel, when there was a large attendance. The secretary, Mr B.G.Evans, introduced the meeting with prayer.

A splendid miscellaneous programme followed:-

Solo - Clarice Hodge	Recitation - Master Verdi James
Solo - Doreen Wilson	Solo - Master Brinley Hodge
Recitation - Vera Wilson	Solo - Florence Phillips
Recitation - Master Robert Davies	Recitation - Mr G. Mathias
Solo - Mr Leslie Phillips	Solo - Katie Thomas
Recitation - Alice Allen	Solo - Lucy Mathias
Duet - Beattie Davies and Katie Thomas	Solo - Annie Hodge
Temperance Hymn - by congregation	Recitation - Mrs Howard James
Duet - Beattie Davies and Katie Thomas	Solo - Muriel Hodge
Recitation - Nellie Allen	Solo - Beattie Davies
Recitation - Pattie Phillips	Solo - Lucy Mathias
Quartette - Mr T. W. Phillips & friends.	

Narberth Weekly News 17 February 1927

New Business - friends of Mr G.H.Phillips, Crafty, are interested to learn that he is shortly opening a boot repairing business at Clynderwen, and all wish him success. *"All work promptly and neatly executed at moderate charges".*

Narberth Weekly News 21 March 1929

(*Tenby Observer 22 Sept 2000 - "The death of Mr George Henry Phillips is recorded at the age of 94 years. He had been a shoe repairer and retail shop proprietor in Clynderwen for many years and his wife had predeceased him by only two months at the age of 92." The paper comments, "the death of this local character sees the end of an era".*)

Trip - the Mothers' Union annual trip took place on Wednesday last week. They journeyed to Swansea for the day by bus which belonged to Messrs Williams Brothers, Laugharne.

Some Family! - a bitch belonging to Ronnie Glanville, West Llanteg Farm, gave birth recently to 18 pups. Is this a record?

Narberth Weekly News 29 June 1933

Young Farmers' Club - Llanteg Y.F.C. held its first social evening on Tuesday last and was most successful.

Narberth Weekly News 17 Jan 1940

Called Up - Mr H. James, son of Mr and Mrs H.James of Blackheath, was called up for service in the Army this week. He, likewise, will carry away with him the best wishes of everyone in the parish.

Narberth Weekly News 18 Jan 1940

New Telephone Subscriber - Mr D.W.Morse Esq., Castle Ely. His number is Llanteg 49.

Narberth Weekly News 6 June 1940

Eileen Oriel née Allen
Photo: Alan Mason

Success - Miss Eileen Allen, Ruel Wall, has been awarded A.L.C.M. after an examination at the London College of Music.

Narberth Weekly News 25 July 1940

A.R.P. Lecture - an instructional lecture was held at Crunwere School on Friday evening last by Mr J.D.Roberts, Narberth Head A.R.P. Warden. The talk was on incendiary bombs, their effects, and methods of dealing with them. Mr Roberts drew sketches which gave splendid illustrations to his remarks. The Rev. D.Morgan presided.

Narberth Weekly News 25 July 1940

Welcome Home - on Tuesday evening of last week there was a 'welcome home' for driver Hugh James, son of Mr and Mrs H.James, Blackheath. There was a large attendance which fully testified to the popularity of Hugh in the district. The Rector, Rev. D.Morgan, presided, and he spoke of the high regard with which Hugh was held by everyone, and how glad he was to see Hugh looking fit and well. The usual gift of 10 shillings was presented to him by Mr F.A.G.Wolff (*presumably Mr F.E.C.Wolff, Headmaster of Crunwere School*) after which he was handed a personal gift by the Chairman from Mrs Morgan, the Rectory, who was unable to attend.

Hugh is in the R.A.'s.

A programme of miscellaneous items followed.

Narberth Weekly News 28 Nov 1940

Welcome Home - on Thursday last a large crowd gathered at the Schoolroom to welcome home Driver Hugh James, R.A., W.O. Desmond Wolff, R.A.F., and John Hayden, Military Police. John Hayden had already been demobilised, Hugh would shortly be discharged and Des would probably be out of the R.A.F. by early August.

Narberth Weekly News 17 Jan 1946

Personal - friends sympathise with Mrs Howard James, Blackheath, who has been confined to her bed for several weeks, and trust that she will make a speedy recovery. Also Miss Ivy Allen, Oxford, who has undergone a minor operation at Haverfordwest Hospital.

Narberth Weekly News 30 May 1946

Victory Celebrations - at a public meeting held at Crunwere Schoolroom on Monday evening of last week final arrangements were made for June 8th. It was decided to hold the children's sports in the afternoon, commencing at 1pm prompt, followed by tea from 4-6pm. After tea there will be sports events for the adults.

Narberth Weekly News 30 May 1946

Celebrations - the celebrations were held in a field kindly lent by Mr York Glanville, West Llanteg Farm. The sports for the children were held in the afternoon, followed by a tea in the field. Food was given by ladies of the district. The adults' sports were held in the evening, when there was keen competition in all events.

A radiogram was lent by Mr Ben Lewis, Amroth, which provided music throughout the day and was also used for the announcements. Light refreshments were served at 8pm and a collection taken to defray the cost of the sports prizes.

Narberth Weekly News 13 June 1946

Sick List - it is pleasing to record that Rev. D.Morgan continues to make excellent progress towards complete recovery after a fairly long and trying illness. Mrs James, Blackheath, who has been laid aside for some time, is also rapidly improving.

Narberth Weekly News 3 Oct 1946

Congratulations - heartfelt congratulations and best wishes to Mr Alfred James, Broomylake, who attained the age of 87 years on Saturday last.

Narberth Weekly News 3 Oct 1946

Young Farmers' Club - the first winter meeting was held last Tuesday evening. Owing to the corn harvest the attendance was small and it was decided that the selection of officers should be deferred to the next meeting.

Narberth Weekly News 17 Oct 1946

Death - the death of Mr William Davies, Stanwell Villa, aged 84 years, removes one of the oldest and most respected residents of the district, where he spent the whole of his life. His rare qualities of kindness, coupled with a lively sense of humour, endeared him to many friends and acquaintances, all of whom deeply feel his loss. A faithful member of Crunwere Church, who until recently rode his bicycle to the morning services. A member of the Parochial Church Council and a School Manager, he also frequently attended the afternoon services at the Baptist Chapel (*Zoar*).

Narberth Weekly News 10 Oct 1946

Mothers' Union - a successful whist drive was held at the Schoolroom recently in aid of Mothers' Union funds. All arrangements were in the hands of Mrs Wilkins, Sandy Grove. During the interval refreshments were provided by the members and friends. Mr Mortimer, Summerbrook, acted as M.C.

Narberth Weekly News 21 Nov1946

For Public Hall - residents are reminded of the whist drive to be held in Tavernspite Village Hall next Wednesday. The proceeds in aid of Llanteg Village Hall.

Narberth Weekly News 5 Dec 1946

Whist Drive - a whist drive was organised by Mrs Hawes at Crunwere School on behalf of the County Hospital. There were 22 tables, the players coming from a wide area.

Narberth Weekly News 5 Dec 1946

Whist Drive - the whist drive organised by Llanteg Hall Committee was held at Tavernspite last Wednesday and was a success. There were 42 tables occupied, whilst a number watched the game. The M.C. was Mr. Hayden Williams, C.C. Narberth, who also gave a handsome donation.

Narberth Weekly News 19 Dec 1946

Dance - on Wednesday evening of last week a very successful dance was held at Llanteg Village Hall. The duties of M.C. were efficiently carried out by Mr R.E.Evans, Llanteglos. He saw to it that a thoroughly enjoyable time was spent by the large number present, which meant that the members of the Melody Makers Band were kept busy. Excellent refreshments were served by the lady members of the committee. During the evening a competition was arranged when a beautifully iced cake, made and given by Miss Margaret Glanville, was won by Mr Kenneth Cole, Beefs Park Farm, Marros.

Narberth Weekly News 26 Feb 1948

Concert - a concert was given by Saunderfoot Male Voice Choir on Friday last, and was arranged by Llanteg A.F.C. in aid of their funds. The programme was a varied and interesting one. Numerous encores being demanded by a large and appreciative audience, who were kept in good humour by the Chairman Mr R.Howells, from Amroth Castle, who also gave a handsome donation to funds. Refreshments were provided by: Mrs R.E.Evans, Miss Millie Phillips, Mrs B.Wilson and Mrs Marwen Phillips, to whom the club send their thanks.

Narberth Weekly News 18 March 1948

Young Farmers - the technical film 'The Science of Milk Production' was shown at Llanteg Hall recently and was very well attended. The meeting was presided over by Mr Rhys Lawrence, who introduced the speaker, Miss M.Jones, of the Dairy Advisory Staff. Numerous questions were put to the speaker at the close, as well as to Mr Davies, Livestock Officer, who was also present.

Narberth Weekly News 1 Apr 1948

Variety Show - despite the rough weather on Friday evening last, all roads over a wide area seemed to lead to Llanteg, where the new Village Hall was once again crowded to capacity to see a really 1st class show (organised by the Crunwere Branch of the W.I.). The performance lasted over two hours, during which time there was not a dull moment. Mrs Noot and everyone who took part deserve the highest praise.

The show was equal to any theatrical performance in larger towns. The advantage of possessing a spacious hall in a rural area, capable of staging such an event, was clearly demonstrated.

Narberth Weekly News 8 Apr 1948

W.I. - despite very cold weather, 21 members were present to welcome the speaker, Mrs Leather, V.C.O. Mrs Leather complimented Llanteg on their growing membership and was especially delighted to see so many young members.

Tenby Observer 21 Jan 1977

For Sale, The Rectory - a beautiful Georgian Country House together with a Coach House converted into two 3-bedroomed flats. Surrounded by one and three-quarter acres of lovely gardens and grounds, and having a five-acre field adjacent. There is a sheltered dell with pond, old well and windmill. The main house consists of six double bedrooms and a single.

Tenby Observer 23 Mar 1977

Jubilee Tree Planting at Llanteg - a Thanksgiving Service was held at the Parish Church on June 5th. Rev. D.S.Hobbs conducted the service which was enjoyed by a good sized congregation. The collection was in aid of Her Majesty's Jubilee Fund.

Tuesday afternoon was given over to sports, for contestants of all ages. Events included tug-of-war pulls, a five-a-side football knock-out match and many other events. An excellent tea was provided for all.

The oldest surviving member of the original Public Hall Commitee, Mr Bill George, planted two trees in the hall grounds: an acer given by Mr Geoff James and a flowering cherry given by S.P.D.C.

A social evening, including dancing, continued until midnight. Mr Peter Blake was in charge of both the sports and evening entertainment. The large number of willing helpers will be thanked at the next meeting of the Crunwere Community Council.

Tenby Observer 17 June 1977

W.I. - 31 members were present at Llanteg Hall. Mrs Deathridge discussed the annual dinner. It was unanimously decided that the proceeds of this year's carol singing should be donated to the Lingfield Hospital School in

Surrey where the grandson of one of the members is a pupil. The remainder of the evening was given over to Christmas festivities.

Tenby Observer 23 Dec 1977

MR GEORGE GIBBS

Photo: Audrey James

L. to R. Friend, Darren, Audrey, George Gibbs and Geoffrey

A former 'gentleman of the road' and well known by many people in Pembrokeshire, Mr Gibbs was featured on a television programme in 1993. He spent over 40 years travelling Wales and will be remembered by many pushing his belongings in an old black pram, walking up to 20 miles a day in search of casual work on farms. One of his old haunts was at Llanteg, where he became friendly with the James family of Rose Park.

WOMEN'S INSTITUTE

by Mollie James

A branch of the Women's Institute was set up in Llanteg in March 1948 under the leadership of Mrs Mabel Hawes of Heatherland. Membership over the years has varied from being in single figures to approaching thirty.

In the early years, meetings, which took place on the first Thursday of each month, were held in the Church Hall (once Crunwere School). It is recorded that at one time members would provide their own heating by purchasing coal and attending to the fire themselves. When the Church authorities sold the old school, meetings were transferred to the new Village Hall; and later on, until the end of 1999, when rising costs and falling membership began causing financial difficulties, they were held in the homes of members.

Llanteg W.I. 1970s **Photo: Eirwen Davies**

Over the years a wide variety of interests have been pursued. Needlework, cookery, flower arranging, first aid and health matters have always been important. Illustrated talks on travel, life in other countries, places and times (particularly from a woman's point of view), demonstrations of silk painting, corn dollies, decoupage and many other skills were ever popular.

In the early 1980s drama was a central project. The group took part in competitions set up by the Pembrokeshire County Federation, appearing with some success at the Torch Theatre, Milford Haven. In 1980 Llanteg performed on stage at the Sherman Theatre in Cardiff in the Welsh Region of the W.I. National 'Scene 80' competition with their own version of 'The Rebecca Riots'.

Many members over the years have taken part in the running of the branch, some following the example of Mrs Hawes and serving on the County Executive. For many years, in turn with our paired institute, a representative has been sent to the A.G.M., held originally at the Albert Hall in London, to vote according to our instructions on the 'Resolutions'.

Sadly, at the end of 1999, due to falling numbers and the lack of volunteers to act as officers, members decided that the Llanteg branch would have to close. In a meeting on 19th July 2000, the club was officially suspended in the presence of two V.C.O.s representing the Pembrokeshire Federation of the W.I.

THE OLD CRAFT OF GRAVE LINING

In former days, the traditional Pembrokeshire practice of lining the inside of graves was an accepted feature of burials in the Llanteg area. Unhappily, rising costs in recent times have literally killed off the craft, and there are few now still alive who remember how it was done.

One such person is Hugh James, of Arfryn. For at least four generations, the Broomylake Jameses, builders by trade, lined graves following this old tradition - Hugh's great-grandfather William James, his grandfather Alfred James, his father Howard James, and Hugh himself.

Hugh recalls that his grandfather's method of working was to build up the lining with stones of even size which he picked from the fields and mortared into place. He topped each grave with a flagstone lid, and for this he charged two shillings and sixpence. When Hugh himself first began the practice, he used bricks, then later on concrete blocks, chamfered at the top. Originally he asked £1 2s 6d, but by the time he retired inflation had forced the cost up to £70.

He has bricked graves not only in Crunwere (Church, Zoar and Mountain) but also Whitland, Marros, Eglwyscymmin, St Florence, Pendine and further afield. There were variations in the depth of graves according to the churchyard and incumbent: some were dug to hold three coffins, one on top of the other. (Incidentally, elmwood lasts much longer than oak, Hugh advises.) He describes how each grave was dug in the shape of a coffin, widest at the shoulders and tapering towards the feet. The bottom was spread with sawdust, and two pieces of wood placed towards either end to raise the coffin off the floor slightly so that the tapes, or ribbons, could be withdrawn smoothly after interment.

The earth at Crunwere is good to dig, says Hugh; but at Ludchurch a small blast was needed to make a decent hole. Worst of all was the sandy soil of Pendine Chapel among the dunes beside the sea. He recalls lining the grave there of a young seventeen-year-old girl tragically killed in a road accident. The sand kept collapsing inward, so he was forced to build up the lining one course at a time, waiting until the mortar was set before beginning a new level. It was dark by the time he had finished, and he was down in the grave working by candlelight.

Another time, when he was inside a deep grave in the early morning dawn at Eglwyscymmin, singing to himself as he worked, he frightened the wits out of a passing roadman who mistook Hugh's voice for a message from the supernatural.

Apart from his work with graves, Hugh James has other lasting connections with Crunwere Church. It was he who made the pointed arch of the porch and embellished it with what Mr Charles F.Shepherd (in his pamphlet *St Elidyr's Church*) describes as "a curiously rustic decoration of flowerheads" impressed in the render. He was also responsible for installing in 1957 the rood beam donated by Paul L.Davies and family; and for moving the font - at the then vicar's request - from its traditional place near the altar to its present one at the rear of the church, a move which necessitated cutting down the base to accommodate it in its new position.

Hugh James is rightly proud of his craftsmanship. The irony is that so much of it will never see the light of day.

WATER

An inspiring poem composed by Mrs Muriel Hellings, Finlandia (d.1999) published in the Tenby Observer on 8th July 1994.
(Reproduced by kind permission of Mr Peter Hellings.)

"Water, water everywhere
And not a drop to drink"
I wonder who it was said that
It makes you stop and think.

Sometimes the rain goes on and on
It doesn't seem to stop
But there's a purpose for it all
We need each little drop.

There's reservoirs to store it
All ready for the days
When sunshine dries up lots of land
With its powerful rays.

The earth was flooded once we know
When Noah built his ark
Since then we've had the rainbow
When stormy skies are dark.

Just think of those in Africa
Crying out in the mid-day sun
For rains to water all their land
And quench their thirsty tongue.

The woman of Samaria
Was shocked when Jesus asked
To give Him water from the well
He did not have a flask!

But Jesus offered her that day
"Life-giving" water, free
He said "You'll never thirst again
If you will come to me".

So thank God for the raindrops
And all the showers too
And pray for "showers of blessing"
To come to me and you.

PART FOUR

REMINISCENCES

PART FOUR: REMINISCENCES

There are still a few people alive today who can remember what village life meant in the early years of the century just gone. It meant knowing and being known by everybody else in the village. It meant finding your entertainment, such as it was, in the village or within walking distance of it. To go anywhere at all was for most country people a treat.

Village People - a hundred years ago it would have meant people who were born in the village, lived all their lives there and died there - in many cases in the same house as their father and grandfather. If you were born in the village you belonged to the village. Things have now changed and we do not have anyone in Llanteg living in the same house in which they were born. The number of residents who were born in the village has also declined sharply with increased mobility, and the continuation of local family connections within the community has all but been severed. During the next decade we will probably see the destruction of almost all the family ties which have stretched back through the generations for centuries in Crunwere, and that is why we feel that it is so important to collect what information we can about our village heritage before it is lost for ever.

"Remember the days of old, consider the years of many generations; ask your father, and he will shew thee; thy elders, and they will tell thee..."

Deutronomy 32/7

M.E.Bevan (nee Davies)

Mrs Betty Bevan was born at Trenewydd. She had two brothers and two sisters and had to share a bedroom when young. Until she was 13 years old she attended Crunwere School, and then went to Narberth Grammar School for a year, cycling from Trenewydd to Kilanow Cross to catch the Narberth bus.

Her favourite lesson was needlework and she recalls playing hopscotch, rounders and skipping at playtimes. In the evenings after school she would help on the farm, and there were occasional whist drives.

Betty recalls that only two or three people locally had cars, therefore the roads were far quieter. Vegetables were grown at home, and groceries could be bought from travelling vans as well as from the local shop at The Laurels. There was also a bakery at Middleton. If people wanted fresh meat, they either slaughtered their own or bought it from Mr Carew, the butcher at Tenby. Because few people had transport, the meat could be ordered in advance and collected from the Ebsworth service bus at Folly Cross.

Pedlars would also call, walking from door to door selling pegs and camping on the roadside. Betty says it was not uncommon to see them camp on the Crosslands road, at the corner of the entrance to Trenewydd lane.

Betty met her husband Ronnie in 1943 and they married in Crunwere Church, going to live at Three Wells. They had eight children and now have twenty grandchildren and three great-grandchildren. At the time of their move to Three Wells there was no electricty, mains water or inside toilet. There was no television either, only a wireless - Betty says they "listened to everything".

She and Ronnie bought their first car in 1952. This was the year that mains electricty came to Tavernspite, when the present primary school was built there. It was also installed at Three Wells. Betty recalls having to go home to Trenewydd to watch the Queen's Coronation in 1953 on her parents' television set.

Regarding the changes she has witnessed in her lifetime, Betty feels that work is a lot easier with electricity and technological improvements, but she would like to see the slower pace of life returning. Two of the biggest changes she has seen are increased traffic and the general trend to a more violent society. She also believes that village life years ago was more friendly because you knew everyone. There are "a lot of strangers in the area now", she says.

Ruth Mary Bevan

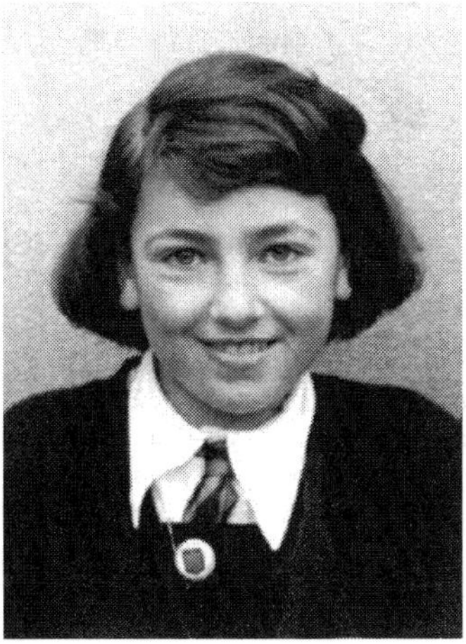

Ruth was born on 7 October 1941 at Cilcwn, Llanmill, Lampeter Velfrey. Her parents were farmers and she had two sisters, with whom she had to share a bedroom when young.

After moving to the Mountain, Ruth attended Llanteg and Amroth primary schools and later Narberth Grammar School. Her favourite subjects were biology, cookery and P.E. At playtimes they would have netball and tennis. In the evenings after school Ruth would do homework, meet her friends and sometimes do chores at home.

She recalls some incidents from her schooldays: going away on Saturdays with the hockey team, waiting for exam results and trying to avoid the Headmaster every morning so as "not to read the lesson in Assembly".

Her favourite meal was a Sunday roast, and her mother also made a special stew with dumplings. Her parents grew some fruit and vegetables and they also shopped at Mrs Bowen's in Llanteg (*The Laurels*).

Transport was mainly buses - Ruth had to walk half a mile to catch the school bus. On occasions she would walk up to three or four miles. She had her first car when she was twenty; her parents did not have one.

She does not recall any birthday parties but remembers having "very small gifts". Christmas was celebrated "at home with my family". There was carol singing and Church concerts, and Ruth would have gifts of "books, clothes, games, and once a bike".

Crunwere Church was attended as a family and it was a big part of her life in her younger days, Ruth says.

The family had a wireless and she enjoyed The Archers, Mrs Dale's Diary, the Afternoon Play and Frankie Howerd. The family had their first TV in the early 1950s, Ruth's favourite programmes being Rawhide, Bonanza, quiz programmes and comedies. They had their first coloured television when Princess Diana got married in 1981.

Ruth met her partner on St Valentine's night in Narberth almost 30 years ago.

She believes that life has changed for the better in lots of ways, but she would like to see the family home life return and to be able to go out without being afraid. She thinks, too, that there should be more discipline for youngsters.

Regarding village life, Ruth states that "years ago everyone helped each other all they could, today you rarely see your next door neighbour and hardly know them".

Kenneth George B.E.M.

Ken was born at The Downs, Llanteg, as was his father, who farmed as well as doing other work. He had three brothers and two sisters (one brother dying at the age of 32) and throughout his childhood had to share a bedroom.

William Henry, Martha James
Photo: Ken George

Ken's father had a brother and two sisters. One sister married William Henry James, but died young. While married they had lived at Manchester House, Tavernspite, but after her death William Henry went to live with his brother at Bevlin. The other sister married someone from Llanddowror and had one child. Tragically however, the whole family died young of T.B. and were buried at Elim Chapel, Llanddowror.

Ken attended Crunwere School and later Tavernspite, leaving at the age of fourteen. He can still recall many of his classmates as well as his teachers - Mr Wolff and Miss Player at Crunwere and Mr Harris in Tavernspite. His favourite subjects were history and maths and he remembers doing P.E. at school "but not often". At playtimes they generally played football.

After school Ken would mostly do work at home: picking stones, weeding the garden, cutting thistles or getting water. "There was no running water when I was young", he says.

He remembers one incident that happened after Sunday School, when a few boys started up a lorry left by the Home Guard and managed to drive it a short way. Unfortunately it got jammed in a gateway and they were unable return it. The owner subsequently "got a ear full from the police for not immobilising it" - an offence in wartime.

Ken's favourite meal from childhood was roast beef and yorkshire pudding. Shopping was mostly done with the Co-op in Kilgetty, while smaller things were bought in Llanteg's Post Office cum shop (*The Laurels*).

A lot of time during the holidays was spent in Tenby with an aunt.

Ken walked to Crunwere and Tavernspite Schools - "what else could we do!" - a distance of about three miles to Tavernspite. He remembers the bus service, and the family having their first car in 1952. They all attended Crunwere Church and Ken would go on a Sunday School outing once a year.

No birthday presents are recalled, but Ken remembers Christmas as "a family time", with concerts held in the school. The family had a wireless, and Ken had his first TV after he married.

He served in the R.A.F., taking part in the Berlin Air Lift, for which he received the Berlin Airlift Medal.

He met his future wife at a motor-cross meeting around 1950 and they married in Ludchurch in 1954.

Ken believes that he is the only Llanteg-born person to be in receipt of both the British Empire Medal and the Imperial Service Medal. The B.E.M. was awarded for services to the public during the floods in Carmarthen in 1989: it was here that he met the Prince and Princess of Wales. The I.S.M. was awarded for 25 years in the Civil Service - altogether Ken went on to serve for 42 years.

He considers that life is now "much better" and thinks that one of the biggest changes over the years has been with transportation - "you can get anywhere these days". This book is a good idea, he says, because "Llanteg has a lot of history and many characters".

Susan James (nee Eggleton)

Susan writes: "I was born in Cardiganshire and it was in November 1961 that my mother and father, Ron and Meg Eggleton, came to live at Ledgerland with myself and my brother Simon.

The memory of our moving-in day is a vivid picture in my mind. The house had not been lived in for some time, fires had been lit to warm and air the place, and whilst we were sitting around the table having supper, an enormous piece of lath and plaster fell from the ceiling, landing right in the middle of the table. I can to this day see the look of horror on the faces of my family and Jack and Graham Mortimer and Freddie Oriel, who had been helping us move in.

Some of the children from the village went to Tenby School, but my brother and I went to Whitland Grammar School. We had to walk up the long rough lane to catch the mini-bus. In winter this meant wearing wellingtons and changing into our school shoes once we reached the top. It was on one of these days that Simon slung his satchel, containing his shoes, over his shoulder and one of the shoes flew out straight through the kitchen window! He made a quick exit, hoping things would have cooled down when he got home.

When we first came to Ledgerland there was no water supply in the house, just a tap outside, and an outside toilet at the bottom of the garden. Neither did we have mains electricity - the electricity we did have was supplied by a generator, which would often run out of fuel, plunging us into darkness. The generator also caused the lights to flicker constantly. It was not until the 1970s that we had mains electricity and the luxury of an indoor bathroom.

Shopping was done at The Laurels and also mobile shops would call. In later years when these vans ceased calling we would have to go to the Co-op in Kilgetty for provisions - as we had no car this was quite an excursion! My mother was a very keen gardener and we would have lots of fruit and vegetables from the garden.

Occasionally we would go by train to visit my grandparents, who lived in London. Sometimes we would go to Tenby or Carmarthen on the service bus.

In our teenage years we joined the Y.F.C. run by Mr Wyn Lawrence and this was great fun, especially when we visited other Y.F.C.s for social evenings. We would sometimes go to Tenby to the pictures - at that time there were two cinemas to choose from. We would travel to Narberth,

Haverfordwest or even Fishguard for a Saturday night dance. By the time we got there it was nearly time to come home again!

Thinking back it is difficult to remember what we used to get up to, but we were never bored, even with no TV. In the summertime we would walk to the beach across Wood-Reefe to Tin-Pits, where we would happily spend the day, only coming home when it was milking time. We had a pedigree Jersey herd of which my father was very proud. He would put milk in cartons and sell it locally (of course this was all before E.U. regulations).

It must have been such a difficult life for my parents who had been brought up in London, which they left following my father becoming a Conscientious Objector during the War.

I met my husband Roy at the Silver Jubilee celebrations in 1977. We married in 1980 at Crunwere Church and now live at Meadowcroft with our son Samuel.

My brother Simon, after many years with Dyfed Powys Police, has now returned to live at Ledgerland with his family, Debi and Leanora."

Kathleen Anne Davies (nee Morse)

Kathleen was born at Castle Ely, Red Roses, of farming parents. She had one brother and two sisters and shared a bedroom when she was small.

Until she was fourteen Kathleen attended Crunwere School, and then went to another school in Carmarthen. Some of her schoolfriends at Llanteg were Nancy Phillips the Folly, Doreen Phelps, Joan Thomas and Lilian Davies. She remembers Mr Wolff and a Miss Jones as teachers at Crunwere and her favourite subjects were reading and singing (she recalls Mr Wolff being very kind and writing to her while she was in hospital and also sending her stamps). The children had P.E. lessons and at playtimes would play hop-scotch and hide and seek. They carried their own lunch to school (sandwiches) and they would make a drink of cocoa - Kathleen recalls her brother Walter scalding his wrist doing this. Later on they had school dinners. Mrs Hughes (Mountain View) and Pattie Phillips (Crafty) were the cooks "and what lovely dinners we had". In the summer the children would go on a Nature Study walk down the lane at the back of the school towards Rose Cottage. "We would always chat to Mrs Allan, Jack and Willie's mother, she was a lovely lady. They had a very nice white rose growing outside the front door, and I would love to smell it". After crossing the stream the children would pick blackberries to take back to school and the cooks would then use them to make stewed blackberry and apple to have with custard the following day.

After school Kathleen would do maths and spelling homework. Then there were the calves to feed and chickens to lock up, and afterwards she would go and play with her friend Lilian. There was also a Young Farmers' Club at that time.

Her favourite meal was roast rabbit with bacon on top, followed by rice pudding. The family shopping was done with Maggie at The Laurels. Pedlars sometimes called at their home.

The children and their mother often went on holiday to Aberystwyth on the train, and they loved to watch Punch and Judy shows there.

The family had their first car in 1938 - a Morris Cowley. They also travelled on Ebsworth buses.

The children walked over a mile daily to Crunwere School and on Saturdays Kathleen and her brother Walter would often have to walk from five to seven miles tending the cattle and sheep.

Their parents attended Elim Chapel, Llanddowror, while the children went to Crunwere Church.

Fondly remembered birthday presents were a black doll that was loved, as well as books and games.

There was a wireless at home and Kathleen recalls listening to Children's Hour and Dick Barton Special Agent (6.45pm). They had their first television in 1961.

She met her future husband at a dance in the Gwalia Hall, St Clears, and they were married at Crunwere Church on 4th April 1959. They had two daughters and a son and now have four grandchildren.

Kathleen considers that life in the village has changed as youngsters now have a choice of things to do, whereas in her own youth they had to make their own games and "would help one another".

The Rescue

Kathleen's brother, Walter Devonald, and her sister, Margaret Eileen, were walking a cow down to Tom 'Commercial' (*The Commercial public house which was just past Kilanow corner*). The noisy arrival of a convoy of Army lorries and tanks frightened the cow, and it stampeded off the roadside and fell into a 30ft ravine. Luckily its fall was broken, but it was left suspended, spreadeagled on the canopy of trees.

Margaret and Walter sat and cried, not knowing what to do. An Army lorry stopped to ask them what was wrong. On hearing about the calamity, the soldiers immediately offered to 'retrieve' the beast, an offer which was gratefully accepted.

The men went down a lane which skirted the ravine, and reaching the cow, slung several ropes around it and hauled it back up to the road.

With just one solitary bruise on the leg to show for its adventure, the cow continued on to its destination.

Noel Hugh Davies

Noel was born at Bryneli Farm on 22nd December 1926. His parents were farmers and he had three brothers and one sister, sharing a bedroom with two of his brothers.

Noel attended Crunwere School until he was ten and then went on to Narberth Grammar School until he was sixteen. He remembers many Llanteg schoolfriends "especially after looking at an old school photo owned by Graham and Jean Mortimer". At playtimes he recalls kicking a ball "or a tin!" around.

Once there was a mass walk-out of pupils from Crunwere School, says Noel: one morning there was a sudden heavy downfall of snow, which was much appreciated by all the children, particularly during the dinner break (sandwiches then - no school meals) when they engaged in snowball fights in the school yard. After a while this became a bit tame, and, aided and abetted by a few ringleaders ("who were they I wonder?!"), everyone crossed the road to the Mountain field opposite, and had a wonderful time sliding down the steep slope on pieces of board. Time stood still, and it was about 2.30pm when the Headmaster, Mr F.E.C.Wolff, finally caught up with his errant pupils and marched them all back to the school! Noel forgets what punishment was meted out to them.

He also recalls a story relating to Mr Wolff which he heard some years after the Second World War. Mr Wolff was a First World War veteran and served in the Llanteg Home Guard during World War Two. An important week-day Home Guard exercise was going to be held and Mr Wolff wrote to his boss, the Director of Education for Pembrokeshire, asking whether he should attend the exercise, or work at the school. The Director (a canny administrator!) replied: "Dear Mr Wolff, I am sure I can rely on you to do your duty".

During the War the school was used for 'Welcome Home' concerts for members of H. M. Forces on leave. Mr Wolff, a fierce patriot, was very proud of his past pupils, and always wanted to know about their life in the Services.

Noel believes that when Mr Wolff retired, he stayed for six weeks with a Welsh-speaking family near Swansea in an attempt to learn the language by "total immersion".

Noel's favourite meal was 'cawl a cig a tatws', and on haymaking and threshing days he enjoyed boiled ham with vegetables followed by rice pudding. He recalls the family having "a first class vegetable garden" and their other shopping needs were met by either 'Maggie the shop', a trip to Whitland, or a van that called weekly ('Idris from Whitland').

Gypsies would come round selling clothes pegs, and there were also some tramps - a pair called Dick and Dolly - and 'Shoni Onions' from Brittany on his bike.

Travelling was done in a pony and trap. Also most people had bikes, including Noel's mother and the District Nurse, Nurse Greenslade. Later they used Ebsworth's buses, and the family had their first car in the late 1930s, an Austin 7, registration number DE 8192.

Noel remembers the Young Farmers' Club was set up in the village either during or just after the Second World War.

He and his three brothers and sister attended Crunwere Church with his mother, who was an active member, but he states that it was not a very big part of his life. His father, who was Welsh speaking, attended Elim Chapel, Llanddowror.

At Christmas Noel remembers going to Church, and the gifts of oranges, nuts and dates in a stocking that was hung up at the bottom of his bed on Christmas Eve. They also celebrated New Year's Day with a special meal, whilst on New Year's morning he would go around the farms singing a carol and wishing everyone "A Happy New Year".

The family had a wireless and they would listen to the News, religious services and the hymn singing.

Noel met his partner in Swansea in 1954 and they were married in 1956. They have three children and one grandchild.

He believes that on the whole life is better now, even though things are more hectic. However he would like to see a "a more law-abiding society". The biggest change he has witnessed has been "the volume and speed of the traffic".

Noel believes that compiling this book is a good idea and he would like to see it including articles about the origins and past history of Crunwere, and also oral history taken from the older inhabitants of Llanteg *(we hope you will be satisfied with the result, Mr Davies! - compiler).*

Mary Evans (nee George)

Photo: Mary Evans

L. to R. Arthur, David, Mary and baby Winifred George, 1941

Mary was born at The Downs, as was her father. She believes she was the last girl to enter Crunwere School before its closure, and for that reason was given a glass-eyed velvet doll on a wicker chair when the school finally closed in 1946. Sadly, the doll was lost when the family home was sold.

Mary enjoyed handicrafts, and as a teenager in the 1950s she made a calico cover for the new organ at Crunwere Church (she trained as a dressmaker with T. P. Hughes of Tenby).

When Mary married she was given a set of silver knives by Millie Phillips, Middleton *(these knives had been in Millie's 'bottom drawer' in the 1920s, but unfortunately her fiancé died and so the contents of the 'bottom drawer' had never been used)*. Mary has now been married almost 42 years and still has the set in the original box.

She remembers people from the village calling her grandfather 'Grandpa George', and there was also 'Granny Glanville' - probably they were two of the oldest people in Crunwere at that time.

Her grandfather, Richard George, believed that what we now call the 'Roman Road', running behind the Hall and Crofty Nurseries, was once a Celtic road, set down very low between the fields so that people were able to move about without being seen as well as providing shelter. Mr George had moved to The Downs in the late 19th century and made handles for scythes and wooden hay rakes etc. for people in the village.

Mary recalls how life has changed: when she was young she would have to attend morning and evening services at Church on Sunday, as well as going to Sunday School in the afternoon. She remembers many Sunday School trips to places as far away as Aberystwyth, Porth Cawl and Barry. There would also be a Sunday School party every Christmas.

Mary attended first Crunwere and then Amroth schools, and remembers visiting the Roman excavations at Trelissy in the early 1950s. She had to sit her Grammar School exam in Whitland Grammar with a class of Welsh speakers.

John Allen Phelps

Allen was born in Kilgetty on 14 September 1934, and has one sister. His father was a labourer and his mother cleaned Crunwere Church, and was the caretaker of Llanteg Church Hall (the Old School).

Allen attended Crunwere School until its closure, then went to Amroth, leaving when he was fifteen years old. He recalls that they had games lessons, and at playtimes they "played a lot of war games" as well as hide and seek and hoops. The girls played games like hop-scotch. In the evenings after school Allen played with his friends, sometimes helping his uncles on their farm.

During the Second World War there was a lot of military activity in the area, and one thing that Allen recalls well were the tanks on Marros Mountain.

He also remembers the Young Farmers' Club and a football team that took part in summer competitions.

Because Allen's childhood was spent during the War, food was in short supply, and therefore he does not recall anything specifically being his favourite. The family had their shopping delivered by the Co-op, while most of their fruit and vegetables were grown in the garden. He doesn't recall going to market very often, but does remember Mr Pomeroy calling and selling clothes.

Allen remembers only one holiday when he was a child and this was to relatives in Cardiff. His family never owned a car and mainly travelled by bus. He walked to school, as well as to places like Tavernspite and Amroth - "you had no choice but to walk", he says. The Sunday School outings were by bus to places like Tenby.

The whole family attended Crunwere Church, which was a big part of their lives.

Christmas was spent "always at home with the family" and they had parties and concerts and carol singing. Allen's father was very clever and made a lot of their toys - "one in particular I remember was a Sunderland flying aircraft".

They had a wireless which was run by two large batteries (one wet and one dry). The wet battery had to be charged up at the local garage. Allen says he enjoyed listening to 'Dick Barton Special Agent' and sports programmes such as cricket, tennis, football and boxing. Their first television was acquired in 1959 and the whole family's favourite programme was 'Coronation Street'.

Allen met his partner at a dance in Saundersfoot in 1961, marrying at Pendine Church in 1963. They have a son and daughter and two grandchildren - "again, a boy and a girl".

Allen has seen a lot of changes in his lifetime, "and not all for the better". He believes it seems that children grow up too quickly, and that "there doesn't seem to be the politeness of yesteryear". The advent of TV, computers etc. has changed how we live, and he considers that people's whole lives now "revolve around the television". Travel too has made the world seem smaller - "people think nothing of travelling all over the world.

When I was young, a trip to Carmarthen on the bus was a major event".

Allen thinks that village life has altered a lot: "the residents in the village are constantly changing, whereas when I was young families didn't seem to move, and hence everyone knew everyone else. Farmers helped each other with hay making and so on. A lot of people didn't have transport of their own and, therefore took an interest in what was going on in their own village".

Constance Mary Scourfield (nee Allen)

Connie was born at Oaklands on 6th August 1921. Her father was a builder and she had a brother and sister.

She attended Crunwere School, leaving at fourteen years of age. She remembers many schoolfriends: Donna Mortimer, Margaret and Marjorie Glanville, Eileen Allan, Betty James and Betty Davies. Her teachers were Mr Wolff, Miss Thomas and Miss Jones (the latter both from Narberth). Connie's favourite lessons were sewing, reading, writing and geography. She recalls P.E. lessons, and at playtimes they would play rounders and cricket. After school she would help in the house and do some reading.

Connie's favourite meal was a roast dinner. Their shopping was done at the village shop, but they "did go to Carmarthen occasionally". She also remembers pedlars calling in the village.

She never went on holidays as a child, although she recalls going on trips by coach. The family's only means of transport were buses, and Connie walked to school.

They all regularly attended Crunwere Church and she states that the church was a big part of her life.

Some birthday gifts that she remembers receiving were books and toys and new clothes. At Christmas there was a school concert, special church services and carol singing, as well as "many gifts".

The family had a radio and listened mostly to music, acquiring a television later on.

Connie met her partner through them both attending church services and concerts. They were married at Crunwere Church on 8 August 1942 and had two daughters and one son. They now have seven grandchildren and nine great-grandchildren (including one set of twins and one of triplets).

Connie moved to Whitland 43 years ago and considers that life in

Llanteg has changed very much - "not many people there I know now".

Sylvia Elizabeth Rogers (nee Collingwood)

Sylvia was an only child born in 1929 at York House. Her father was the local roadman.

She attended Crunwere School until fifteen years old and recalls many friends there, her favourite subject being maths. They did P.E. and at playtimes played rounders, cricket and football. After school the evenings were spent mainly at home, although there were a few clubs in the Schoolroom.

Sylvia's favourite meal was boiled ham. The family grew their own cabbage and potatoes. She doesn't recall visiting any markets but remembers "quite a few" pedlars calling at the house.

They had no car, and holidays were spent in Kidwelly with her father's brothers, travelling there by bus.

Sylvia walked to school as well as to Crunwere Church, and later on walked about four miles daily to work.

There were no birthday parties and not many Christmas gifts - "just what my parents could afford".

She met her partner in 1946 at Crunwere Church and was married there in 1952. They had one child and two grandchildren.

Sylvia considers that life has changed, "not for the better". She only knows a few of the older people in the village now: "we all used to be friends years ago and know everyone".

Marjorie Thomas (nee Glanville)

Marjorie was born at West Llanteg Farm on 5 July 1924. Her parents were farmers and she had three brothers, and never had to share a bedroom.

She attended Crunwere School until 14 years of age. Her friends were Betty Davies, Trenewydd, Vena Owen, Donna Mortimer, Summer Brook, Eileen Allen, Ducy and Valmai Herbert, and Connie Allen, Oxford. Marjorie's teachers were Mr Wolff, Miss Jones and Miss Molly Garrett. They had P.E. lessons and at playtimes did hop-scotch, rounders and skipping. The evenings after school were mostly taken up with farm work and Marjorie attended the Young Farmers' Club in the village.

Her favourite meals were cawl, pork faggots, minced pork and currant pie. Family shopping was done at The Laurels with Maggie Bowen (nee Morris) and swede, cabbage, potatoes and cauliflower were grown at home. Pedlars would call selling lace and pegs.

In the holidays Marjorie cycled over to stay with an aunt at Great Newton, Llanddowror. At other times travelling was done either in a pony or governess cart or on their bikes. The family had their first car around 1951.

They attended Crunwere Church three times on a Sunday: Morning Service, Sunday School in the afternoon, and Evening Service. Mountain Chapel was also attended and Marjorie went to the Temperance meetings there where they had singing and recitations. School and Sunday School trips were to places like St. David's or Tenby.

She does not recall any birthday gifts, but remembers receiving a doll and a stocking full of nuts with an apple and orange at Christmas. The family always enjoyed a traditional Christmas dinner of goose.

They had a radio at home and got their first television in the 1950s.

Marjorie met her partner in 1942 and married in Crunwere Church in 1948. They have one daughter and two grandchildren.

She believes that nowadays the biggest changes have been with transport, traffic and communications, and "the pace of life is much faster". Previously there used to be horse-drawn transport with hardly any cars. There are very few old "village" families remaining, Marjorie says, and it is becoming an impersonal community - "everyone is too busy getting on with their own lives".

John Tunster

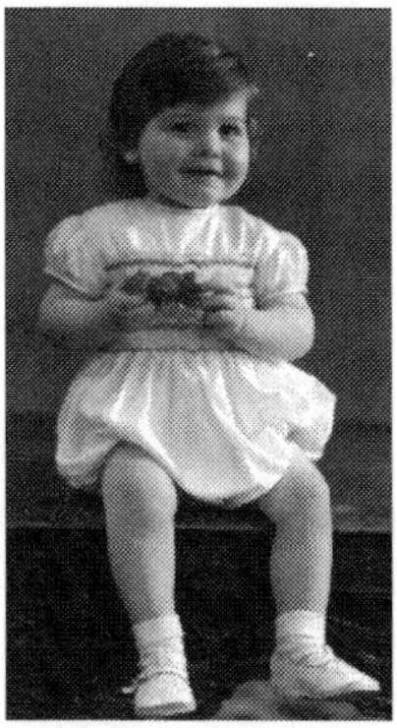

John was born in Haverfordwest in 1968. His father was a farm worker and later a builder, and John himself was brought up at The Factory, Amroth, until he was eight, then went to live at Beech Lea, just outside the parish boundary. He has a sister and had to share a bedroom until he went to Greenhill School at eleven years of age.

John first attended Amroth School, and left Greenhill when he was seventeen. There were forty children in Amroth in two classes, and 25 to 30 a class in Greenhill. The head teacher at Amroth was Mr Bernard Williams. John liked most of the subjects taught, especially art, computers and music. He enjoyed the music and movement classes at Amroth but states that he hated rugby, gym and athletics at Greenhill although "swimming and tennis were O.K.". He recalls that during his first week at Greenhill the whole class, including the teacher, spent half a lesson trying to find a classroom that hadn't been built!

In the evenings after school John would meet with friends at Llanteglos where they had a tree-house and a rope swing. There were Cubs and Scouts in Kilgetty, but by this time the Young Farmers' Club had finished in Llanteg.

John recalls scrap metal being collected by gypsies.

Holidays were spent with family in Gloucester and in London with friends.

John's parents always had a car. He had to catch two buses to get to school and sometimes he would cycle to Tavernspite or Kilgetty. He attended Glanrhyd Chapel with his father and Crunwere Church with his mother.

He remembers having 'traditional' birthday parties, with jelly and ice cream, sausage rolls and pineapple on sticks, and playing games such as Musical Chairs, Blind Man's Buff and Pass the Parcel.

The early television programmes that John enjoyed were Coronation Street, Z Cars and The Good Life. He also liked listening to The Archers and the music charts on the radio.

John believes that the main ways in which things have changed during his lifetime have been that there are no longer "jobs for life" and that there is a lot more divorce. The biggest personal change in his life was "going away to work for five years in London".

He considers this book is an excellent idea because "if this information is not recorded now it will be lost forever".

Olive Williams (nee Roberts)

Olive's grandmother Susanna was the fourth daughter of Susan and George Scourfield *(see The Scourfield Family of Llanteg elsewhere in this book).*

Mrs Scourfield would do her shopping in Whitland, travelling there by pony and trap which she drove herself. She would also take her grandchildren to the beach at Amroth in the trap. Usually four grand-daughters would go on holiday to her at a time and they would all sleep in the same bed, two at the top and two at the bottom.

When Olive was a child in the early 1950s her grandmother would take her on the bus to Kilanow Cross, and from there they would walk to the Mountain Chapel to put flowers on the family graves. This happened about six times a year. They would call in for tea either with Mr and Mrs James of Blackheath or the Misses Phillips of Middleton, and then walk back to the little house on Kilanow Cross (*the old Toll House*) which was just one room as far as Olive can remember. If it rained she and her grandmother would be invited into the house to shelter until the bus came from Tenby, and she would have to sit on a cushion on top of a commode. Olive says she can still recall the smell and how she used to pray that it would be dry weather so that they would not have to go in!

In those days visiting the Mountain Chapel would take all day, but now when Olive visits the graves it takes her only half an hour.

David Vale

David recalls that when he first moved down to Llanteg in the 1960s to work at Trenewydd he lived at Middleton.

After moving into the Folly he would often stop and chat to Mr Wilkins at Sandy Grove. Sometimes Mr Wilkins would hail him on his way back in to work from lunch, and if Mr Wilkins rested his leg (which was very stiff) on the tractor step, David knew that they would be in for a long conversation! As a result he would be late back into work, but never got into trouble as long as he explained to Mr Davies Trenewydd that he had been detained by 'Mr Winka'.

David says that the field names in Trenewydd are pretty much the same as in the 1842 Tithe Map, but that one field then known as the Square Field is now called York Field. This change came about at the beginning of the 20th century when the land was rented out to York Glanville, whose name has stayed associated with the field ever since.

Vaughan Wilson

Vaughan was born in Rhosgoch, Red Roses, on 4 January 1928. His parents were farmers and he had a brother and sister.

Vaughan attended Crunwere School, and later Narberth County School, leaving at the age of 14. He recalls many school friends, and says that his favourite lesson was history. At playtime they would play football. In the evenings after school Vaughan had to help on the farm besides doing homework.

The family grew some vegetables and shopped both in Whitland and in the local shop. Pedlars called quite often.

There were no holidays spent away from home, and transport was mostly by bicycle until the family had their first car in 1938. Vaughan remembers school trips by bus, and also the school party and carol singing at Christmas time. The family all attended Crunwere Church.

They had a radio and listened mostly to the News. A television was acquired in the late 1950s.

Vaughan met his partner in Llanteg in 1955 and they married in Calne, Wiltshire, four years later. They have three children.

Alwyn James

Alwyn lived at Bevlin until the age of 21 when he married and left home. He recalls that in the 1940s he knew most of the residents in Llanteg. Hardly anyone sold up their farms in those days, and properties were passed down through the generations.

Village life consisted of everyone helping each other, especially with haymaking, corn reaping, threshing, potato planting and picking. Together with Leslie Phillips of Middleton, Alwyn would pick potatoes for Leslie Williams at Crunwere Farm; and there were also well-known local gipsies from Kingsmoor Common who helped with the potatoes year after year. During harvesting the work would often go on late into the evening, but there would be a fine spread awaiting the workers: Alwyn remembers that East and West Llanteg Farms especially always put on "a fantastic table of food".

He recalls Willie Allen, Rose Cottage, was the village postman, doing his rounds on his bike and always whistling away, but "not with much tune!"

Reggie Glanville's garage at Llanteg Cross was a regular meeting-place where folk would stop and chat while buying paraffin or getting their 'accumulator' batteries charged. There were a lot of old signs there, including a large globe which proclaimed 'Power Petrol 1/6 a gallon' (this was when the price of petrol didn't change from day to day). Reggie's sister Winnie (at Fern Villa) brewed tea for him every morning and afternoon, and she would let him know when it was ready by blowing a whistle. If Alwyn happened to be at the garage he would often go and fetch the tea, which he recalls was always in a brown jug.

He attended first Crunwere School, and later Amroth. Mrs Lewis, Penglyn, Amroth, drove the transport to Amroth School - an old ex-Army V8 Pilot staff car. Auntie Annie, as she was known, was a keen follower of the Amroth Seagulls football team. At this period Llanteg, too, had a football team and they and their supporters would be transported to matches in Andrew Howells's cattle lorry. The team played and practised in a field near Trenewydd, and also at West Llanteg Farm. Joe Morgan of Craig-y-Borion was the David Seaman of his time!

Often on Sundays Alwyn would walk across Marros Mountain with his grandmother to church. She had many relatives and friends at Marros, and the two of them often went to someone's house for tea after the service. At other times they would travel to Marros via Red Roses and Syke Farm, stopping at Pwllgreen to visit Alwyn's great-uncle.

He recalls that there was a "water pump" set by the side of the road between Bevlin and The Laurels. It had a concrete base but no handle. The domed top could be lifted up to reveal a ball screw which could be turned.

It was quite a substantial structure made of cast iron. Alwyn is not sure whether it was connected to the mains or not, but says he cannot recall a well in that particular area.

It was not uncommon for the monthly meetings of the Llanteg Hall Committee to be held in the kitchen at Bevlin, especially through the winter months. Wilfred Davies of Milton is recalled as being very active in Hall affairs - "the captain of the ship". Mr Davies, together with his wife and son Alan, was an accomplished organist, and Alwyn remembers one memorable Sunday when the three of them were each playing the organ in different chapels (Zoar, Lanteague and Sardis).

On New Year's Day, Alwyn says, he and David George would go together round the parish singing to the householders, often walking up as far as Three Wells and Broomylake.

Reverend Bowen-Harries

The Reverend Isambard George Horatio Bowen-Harries was Rector of Crunwere from 1948 to 1955. He was a Welsh speaker, and had a little corgi dog called Dai which he always addressed in Welsh and which travelled everywhere with him in the car. Unfortunately, one day the dog wandered off and was knocked down and killed on the main road near Llanteg Cross.

When Alwyn arrived home at Bevlin after work his gran told him that Mr Bowen-Harries had a job for him to do. He went to the Rectory, where he found the Rector "pretty upset" as he lived there on his own and the little dog had been his sole companion. He showed Alwyn where to dig a grave, just outside the first window on the right facing seaward, where he would be able to look out and see it. When Alwyn was down to what he thought was a reasonable depth, he stopped; but he says Mr Bowen-Harries wasn't content until the grave was much deeper, because he didn't want poor Dai ever to be dug up by anyone.

The little dog was wrapped in the tartan car rug on which it had enjoyed so many travels with its master, and was buried in a very dignified manner.

APPENDIX

A TABLE OF TOLLS, 1881.

The following is a copy of a table of road tolls which is on display at Colby Lodge.

Pembrokeshire County Roads Board
No. 25 Killanow-Gate
A Table of Tolls
Payable under the Statutes 7 & 8 VICT. c91, & 24 & 25 VICT. c70

For every Horse or other Beast drawing any Coach, Chariot, Berlin, Landau, Landaulet, Barouche, Chaise, Phaeton, Vis-a-Vis, Calash, Curricle, Car, Chair, Gig, Hearse, Caravan, Litter, or any such-like Carriage 0.0.6
For every Horse or other Beast (except Asses) drawing any Waggon, Wain, Cart, or other such-like Carriage 0.0.4
For every Ass drawing any Cart, Carriage or other Vehicle 0.0.2
For every Horse or Mule, laden or unladen and not drawing 0.0.1½
For every Ass, laden or unladen and not drawing 0.0.0½
For every Drove of Oxen, Cows, or neat Cattle, the sum of Ten-pence per Score and so in proportion for every greater or less number
For every Locomotive drawn or impelled by Steam or other Power other than Animal Power, for every Two Tons or fractional part of Two Tons of its weight 0.0.4
And for every Carriage drawn or propelled by such Locomotive per wheel 0.0.4
One-half only of the above Tolls is payable for and in respect of any Horse or other animal employed in carrying, drawing or conveying any Lime, to be used for the purpose of Manure.
A TICKET at this Gate will clear Lanteague, Begelly, Redberth, Tenby, and Catershook Gates, and Killanow Bar.

VILLAGERS WHO SERVED IN THE TWO WORLD WARS

Men of the parish and district who died in the Great War 1914-18:-

Davies William, Private, Bevelin
Glanville H.S., Private, Lanteg

Men killed in action in the Second World War 1939-45:-

Owen L.G.J., S.O. R.A.F, Syke Farm
Mason J., A.B. R.N., Ruel Wall

Men who served their country in the First World War:-

Allen W.T.	Private	Rose Cottage
Beynon William	Driver	Gorse
Callen A.	Private	Longlane
Callen W.	Driver	Longlane
Connol William	Private	Greenacre
Collingwood William	Private	Three Wells
Davies J.	Private	Blackheath
Glanville L.	Private	Lanteg
Glanville R.	Engineers	Lanteg
George R.G.	Private	Downs
Hodge A.	Private	Barriets
Howells William	Private	Woodreef
James B.	Private	Cabin
James C.	Gunner	Summer Brook
James F.	Private	Cabin
James H.	Gunner	Blackheath
James J.	Corporal	Ruel Wall
James T.	Corporal	Ruel Wall
James William	Gunner	Broomy Lake
James William H.	Corporal	Cabin
Jones G.S.	Private	Heatherland
Jones H.	Private	Heatherland
Jones N.G.	2nd Lieut.	Heatherland
Lewis J.	Private	Barn
Lewis T.	Private	Folly
Mortimer J.S.	Sergeant	Ledgerland
Phillips A.G.	Private	Corner
Phillips D.	Gunner	Corner
Phillips T.D.	Captain	Crafty

Phillips T.W.	Sapper	Corner
Phillips William	Driver	Corner
Phillips W.C.	Private	Crafty
Reynolds S.	Driver	Belle Vue
Scourfield J.	L. Corp.	Pantglas

Men and women who served their country in the Second World War:-

Allen N.	L.A.C.	Oxford
Brinsden A.H.	Corporal	Stanwell
Bevan K.	L.A.C.	Brownslade
Davies W.H.	Driver	Brynely
Davies N.H.	Corp. R.A.C.	Brynely
Davies E.G.	Corp. R.A.C.	Brynely
Eyden J.	Private	Syke Farm
George A.	L.A.C.	Downs
Glanville H.R.	Driver	Lanteg West
Hawes Miss M.	A.T.S. Subaltern	Heatherland
Howells A.	Driver	The Valley
Jones N.J.G.	Colonel	Heatherland
Jones G.S.G.	Major	Heatherland
James W.H.	Gunner	Blackheath
James H.R.	L.A.C.	Blackheath
James W.G.	Gunner	Bevlin
James H.G.	Gunner	Bevlin
Mortimer Miss D.	W.A.A.F	Summer Brook
Oriel A.	Driver	Garness
Owens V.M.	R.A.F.	Syke Farm
Phelps G.	A.C.	Milton Back
Williams G.	Capt.	Lanteglos
Williams Mrs R.	Red Cross	Lanteglos
Wolff T.	S. African Navy	School House
Wolff Miss S.	W.A.A.F. Section Officer	School House
Wolff D.	W.O. R.A.F.	School House
Wolff Miss K.	W.A.A.F.	School House

(Taken from the Roll of Honour in Crunwere Church)

BIBLIOGRAPHY

Crunwere Roll of Honour - Crunwere Church
Papers from Dyfed Archaeological Trust
Hearth Tax 1670 - Haverfordwest Record Office
Land Tax 1787 - Haverfordwest Record Office
Census Returns 1841-1891 - Haverfordwest Record Office
Crunwere Church Burial Register - Haverfordwest Record Office
1911 Land Tax - Haverfordwest Record Office
1897 Parish Magazine - Wilson Museum, Narberth
Crunwere School Minute and Log Books - Haverfordwest Record Office
Ordnance Survey Maps 1809 onwards
Narberth Weekly News 1923 - National Newspaper Library, London
Narberth Weekly News 1924 onwards - Tenby Library and National Library of Wales
Narberth Weekly News 1940s and 1970s - Tenby Library
St. Elidyr, Crunwere - a Historical Note Mr Charles F.Shepherd 1933
Young Farmers' Club papers - Mr Wyn Lawrence
Description of Pembrokeshire George Owen of Henllys 1603
A Historical Tour Through Pembrokeshire Richard Fenton 1803
Life and Traditions in Rural Wales J. Geraint Jenkins Aldine Press Ltd 1976
Pembrokeshire County History Volume 111 Pembrokeshire Historical Society
Pembrokeshire Past and Present Brian John Greencroft Books 1995
Oxford Companion to Local History 1996 O.U.P
Correspondence from Mr B.H.J.Hughes, Pembroke Dock
Family Tree Magazine December 1999
Papers relating to Llanteg Poor House 1857 - Haverfordwest Record Office
Abstract of Lease for Oaklands 1884 - Haverfordwest Record Office
Table of Tolls, Colby Lodge National Trust
Also personal papers in private hands